THE INDEPENDENT GUIDE TO WALT DISNEY WORLD 2019

G. Costa

Limit of Liability and Disclaimer of Warranty:
The publisher has used its best efforts in preparing this book, and the information provided herein is provided "as is." Independent Guides and the author make no representation or warranties with respect to the accuracy or completeness of the contents of this book and specifically disclaim any implied warranties of merchantability or fitness for any particular purpose and shall in no event be liable for any loss of profit or any other commercial damage, including but not limited to special, incidental, consequential, or other damages.
Please read all signs and safety information before entering attractions, as well as the terms and conditions of any third party companies used. Prices are approximate, and do fluctuate.

Copyright Notice:
Contents copyright © 2012-2019 Independent Guides. All rights reserved. No part of this document or the related files may be reproduced or transmitted in any form, by any means (electronic, photocopying, recording, or otherwise) without the prior written permission of the publisher, unless it is for personal use. Some images and text are copyright © The Walt Disney Company and affiliates and subsidiaries. This guide is not a Disney product, not is it endorsed by said company, or any other companies featured herein.

Contact us:
If you have questions about this book or the resort, get in touch via our website at www.independentguidebooks.com - we are happy to help.

Contents

1: Introduction	4
2: Planning Your Trip	5
3: Getting There	6
4: Disney Transportation	8
5: Hotels	10
Disney Resort Hotels	12
On-Site Non-Disney Hotels	31
6: Tickets	35
Understanding Ticket Types	35
Ticket Tips	36
Annual Passes	37
7: Magic Kingdom Park	38
Main Street, U.S.A.	40
Frontierland	42
Liberty Square	44
Adventureland	46
Fantasyland	48
Tomorrowland	54
Live Entertainment	57
Parades	58
Fireworks	59
8: Epcot	60
Future World	62
World Showcase	66
More about Epcot	74
Epcot Live Entertainment	74
Illuminations: Reflections of Earth	75
9: Disney's Hollywood Studios	76
Hollywood Boulevard	78
Sunset Boulevard	79
Animation Courtyard	81
Echo Lake	82
Commissary Lane	83
Grand Avenue	83
Toy Story Land	84
Star Wars: Galaxy Edge	85
Live Entertainment	85
10: Disney's Animal Kingdom Park	86
Discovery Island	88
DinoLand U.S.A.	89
Africa	90
Rafiki's Planet Watch	91
Asia	92
Pandora: World of Avatar	94
Live Shows	95
11: MyMagic+	96
12: Fastpass+	97
How to make Fastpass+ reservations	98
What rides should I make Fastpass+ reservations for?	102
Getting those 'hard to get' Fastpasses	102
13: Park Touring Strategies	103

14: Blizzard Beach Water Park	106
15: Typhoon Lagoon Water Park	109
16: Disney Springs	111
17: Guests with Disabilities	118
Disability Access Service (DAS)	119
18: Activities outside the Parks	120
ESPN Wide World of Sports	120
Miniature Golf	120
Golf	121
Free activities outside the parks	122
19: Meeting the Characters	125
Character Dining	127
20: Doing Disney on a Budget	128
21: Dining	130
Disney Dining Plans	130
Reservations and Cancellations	132
Dress Codes	132
22: Useful to Know	133
Photopass and Memory Maker	133
On-ride Photos	134
Single Rider Queue Lines	134
Extra Magic Hours	135
When to Visit	136
Rider Switch	137
Useful Phone Numbers	139
Height Restrictions	139
23: How to spend less time waiting in lines	140
24: Guided Tours	142
VIP Tour Services	146
25: 2019 Seasonal Events	147
26: 2019 and The Future…	152
27: Comparing the Walt Disney World Resort and the Disneyland Resort	154
Ride and Attraction Comparisons	158
28: A Special Thanks	160
29: Park Maps	161

Chapter One | Introduction

Introduction

Walt Disney opened Disneyland in California in 1955 – here Disney fans could meet their favorite characters, families enjoyed time together, and dreams came true every day.

The park was a great success, but as Disneyland was built in a residential area, other hotels and shops started to surround the park with guests seeing billboards towering from inside the park and the illusion of an imaginary world was easily broken.

In the 1960s, Walt Disney developed his "Florida Project", a hugely expanded version of Disneyland. Disney began to secretly buy up part of central Florida bit by bit – 47 square miles of it; this was the beginning of "Disney World".

Sadly, in 1966, Walt Disney passed away and the plans for Disney World almost collapsed. Despite the loss of its founder, the company built Walt's dream, and in

1971 Magic Kingdom Park was unveiled. This park was based on Disneyland, but on a grander scale.

In 1982, Epcot became the second theme park. It is a place to learn about the future, and to visit pavilions representing countries from around the world.

In 1989, Disney's Hollywood Studios became the third theme park – here guests can experience rides and shows inspired by movies.

Finally, in 1998 the fourth theme park opened - Disney's Animal Kingdom Park - where guests can learn about animals, venture on a safari and go on wild rides.

As well as theme parks, Walt Disney World contains two water parks, golf and mini-golf courses, 30 Disney resort hotels, horse-riding areas, backstage tours, spas, shopping and entertainment districts and much more. It really is a Disney world.

You could spend several weeks at the Walt Disney World Resort; it is immense in scale and unimaginable until you experience it.

Acronyms in this book:

Animatronic – The robots you will see in the rides and shows throughout the park.
Attraction – The general term for a ride, character meet, or show at the theme parks.
Boat Launches – Boats from certain Disney resort hotels to theme parks and other locations.
Cast Member (CM) – A Disney employee.
Character Dining – A meal where Disney characters make appearances and visit each table to meet guests and take photos.
Disney Resort – A Disney hotel. They are called resorts because of their elaborate theming and amenities.
Disney Springs – The shopping district of Walt Disney World Resort.
Fastpass+ (FP+) – A free service to save you time waiting in line. We have a dedicated chapter.
Guest – You, the person entering the theme park – you are not a mere visitor, but a guest!
Motorcoaches – Disney's wording for a bus or a coach.

Chapter Two | Planning Your Trip

Planning Your Trip

Planning your trip is single-handedly the most important part of your vacation. We will stress this: your trip does need to be planned. With decisions to make on hotels, park tickets, transportation, dining options, rides, show and attractions it can be a daunting task. Use this page as a checklist to guide you in the right direction.

1. When do you want to visit? – See our "Seasonal Events" chapter to decide the best time for you. Prices and crowds vary depending on the timing of your visit.

2. How are you getting to Walt Disney World? – Driving, flying or public transport? See our "Getting There" chapter for information. Reserve rental cars, shuttles, or Disney Magical Express if necessary.

3. Choose your tickets – Answer these questions to choose a ticket:
• How long will you visit the parks? (We recommend at least one day per park)
• Do you want to visit multiple parks on the same day? (If so, get the "Park Hopper" add-on)
• Do you want to visit the water parks or play mini-golf? (If so, get the "Water Park Fun + More" add-on)

4. Choose a place to stay – An on-site Disney hotel offers perks, but if you will not use these then you can save money by staying at a non-Disney hotel. See our Hotels section to find the best hotel for you. We also cover other nearby Non-Disney hotels.

5. Choose a Dining Plan – If you are staying at a Disney hotel, decide whether you want to pre-pay for your dining. If so, see our Dining section for the different Dining Plan options.

6. Reserve restaurants – If you want to dine at a Table Service restaurant, make your dining reservations up to 180 days in advance by calling 407-WDW-DINE, or on online (more in our Dining section).

7. Study the park maps and read this book – Find our in-park maps at the end of this guide. Note down attractions you want to experience, bookmark pages, and make notes of our Top Tips.

8. Make Fastpass+ (ride and show) reservations – Guests who pre-purchase tickets can use Fastpass+ to reserve rides and shows before arrival. Learn how and why you need to make your reservations in the "Fastpass+" chapter.

9. Plan when you will visit each park – You should know what days you will visit each park. Then, you to make Fastpass+ reservations, decide where to eat, and check park opening hours.

10. Read our Park Touring Strategies chapter – Follow the tips in this chapter, to reduce your waits drastically.

Off-Property – Everything outside of Walt Disney World Resort's land.
On-Property – Everything that is within Walt Disney World Resort's 47-square miles of land.
Queue Line – Sometimes called a "queue", sometimes a "line", and other times a "queue line". These are all interchangeable and mean the waiting area before a ride, restaurant or show.
Quick Service – Refers to dining. This means fast food.
Standby Line – The regular queue line for attractions for guests without a Fastpass+ booking.
Table Service – Refers to dining. This means a full-service restaurant, where food is brought to your table by a waiter or server.
The Magic Kingdom, Magic Kingdom and **Magic Kingdom Park** – These terms are all used interchangeably and mean the first theme park to open at the resort in 1971, which has Cinderella Castle at its center.
Transportation and Ticket Centre (TTC) – An area located next to the Magic Kingdom Park's car parking lot. When arriving by car, you must go through the TTC to get a monorail or boat to Magic Kingdom Park. A monorail service is also available from the TTC to Epcot.

Chapter Three | Getting There

Getting There

Getting to the Walt Disney World Resort, located just outside of Orlando in Florida, is easy – whether you are flying, driving or using public transport, we cover the best ways to get to the resort.

Flying

There are numerous airports that you can fly into. Here we cover the three main locations:

Orlando International Airport (MCO) is our recommended airport – it handles national and international flights, offers numerous transfer options and is less than 25 miles from the Walt Disney World Resort. At the airport, you can hire a rental car, use a shuttle service or taxi, or take advantage of the Disney Magical Express service.

• **Rental cars** – There are many rental car companies at MCO, and Orlando is the largest rental car market in the world. Most of the major car rental companies are located on-airport property. Rental car companies are located in both terminals on the Ground Transportation Level (Level 1). Companies at the airport include: Alamo, Avis, Budget, Dollar Car Rental, Enterprise Rent-A-Car, E-Z Rent A Car, Firefly Car Rental, Hertz Car Rental, National and Thrifty.

• **Driving directions to Walt Disney World**: At the airport, follow Jeff Fuqua Blvd towards FL-417 S (a toll road with a cost of about $2.50). Follow signs to I-4/Tampa/Disney World. About 10.6 miles later take Exit 6 for International Drive. Drive onto FL-536 W / World Center Drive. You are now in the Walt Disney World area; follow signs towards your hotel from here. The total distance is about 20 to 25 miles and about 25 to 40 minutes.

• **Shuttles** – These small buses generally cost $16 to $22 per person one-way to locations on Disney World property. These may be shared with other people. Return trips are around $36 to $40 per person. You will find shuttles from Mears (407-423-5566) at the airport.

• **Taxis and Uber** – These work out cheaper than shuttles for large groups (up to 9 people) and you get the vehicle to yourself. All taxi fares are metered and pricing should be about $60 to $70 one-way to the Walt Disney World Resort. An Uber will usually cost $35-$40 one-way.

• **Disney Magical Express** – This is a complimentary return service from Orlando International Airport to Disney hotels available exclusively to Disney hotel guests. This service is available for both domestic and international guests. On the return journey, guests can even check-in for their flight (selected airlines only) at their hotel. More information is provided when booking the service with Disney online or on the phone.

Orlando Sanford Airport (SFB) – This airport is located 43 miles from the Walt Disney World Resort and is where many international chartered flights fly into, as well as some national airlines. There is no complimentary Disney Magical Express service from this airport. Your options here are:

• **Rental Cars** – These companies have offices based on airport property: Advantage, Alamo, Avis, Budget, Dollar, Enterprise, Hertz, National and Thrifty. We recommend you check and compare rates from various providers as these can vary greatly.

• **Driving directions** (tolls apply): Join and follow FL-417 North for approximately 3.3 miles, take the I-4 West towards Kissimmee. After 39.5 miles on the I-4 you will be in the Walt Disney World area. Follow local Disney signs. Total drive: 43 miles, and about 45 to 50 minutes.

• **Shuttles** – Orlando Carriers, Inc. (407-418-0513) is listed on the official Sanford Airport documentation as providing a shuttle service. Alternatively, Orlando Shuttle Service (orlandoshuttleservice.com) allows you to compare

Getting There

and book various providers online. We have not used either service and cannot make recommendations. The price is approximately $50 per person each way for a shuttle.
• **Taxis and Uber** – The cost is about $100 to $130 each way from the airport to the Walt Disney World Resort. There are often discounts for booking a round-trip fare. Mears Transportation (http://www.mearstransportation.com) is the recommended company at the airport. An Uber will cost about $45 to $55.
Miami International Airport (MIA) – If you are flying into here be prepared for a long transfer time as the airport is about 230 miles away from Walt Disney World, (3.5 hours of driving). Unless you get an incredible deal on flights, the savings in airfare are soon eliminated by the cost of transfers and lost time. There are no widely advertised shuttle services that we know of from the airport to Walt Disney World. As such, your options are:
• **An Internal Flight** – Catch an internal flight from Miami International Airport (MIA) to Orlando International Airport (MCO). The flight time will be one hour.
• **Rental Car** – On arrival at the airport you will need to take a shuttle to the Rental Car Centre. Several rental car companies operate: Advantage Rent A Car, Alamo, All Day Car Rental, Avis, Budget, Dollar, Enterprise, E-Z Rent A Car, Firefly Car Rental, Hertz, National, Payless, P&P Family Auto Rental, Royal, Sixt Rent A Car, and Thrifty.

Rail

Although cross-country public transport is far from world-class in the United States, there are a few options. You can travel from most cities in the North East of the US to Orlando, Florida by Amtrak trains in 18 to 24 hours. This can be a less stressful way of travelling than flying or driving, but is also much slower. Dining coaches are available on long distance Amtrak trains.

Cross-country trips are more complicated and we encourage you to visit the Amtrak website (amtrak.com) for details. From Orlando's Amtrak station you will need a taxi or Uber to Disney World.

Example pricing scenario: A round-trip journey from New York Penn Station to Orlando, Florida booked 10 weeks in advance for January costs $117 for a saver seat, $146 for one adult in a "value" coach seat. A flexible fare is more expensive at around $320.

The same journey in a "roomette" with some meals included, as well as complimentary newspapers and a bed to sleep in costs $375 for one person, or $520 for two sharing.

Driving

We could not possibly tell you how to drive to Walt Disney World from every destination across the US, but it is, of course, a popular option. It is equally possible to drive across the US from a bordering country too.

During peak seasons, especially, you can save thousands of dollars by driving instead of flying. The cost is similar no matter how many people are in the car.

A vehicle also gives you greater freedom: you do not need to wait for buses or shuttles, and if you fancy visiting a supermarket to get food and make a meal, or

Chapter Four | Disney Transportation

Disney Transportation

The Walt Disney World Resort is a large destination with many different forms of transport including boats, buses, ferries and monorails. Here's how to get around the 47 square mile resort.

To Magic Kingdom Park:
From Epcot: Catch the Epcot Monorail at the Transportation and Ticket Center (TTC). There, get the Express Monorail (quicker) or the Resort Monorail (slower) to Magic Kingdom.

From Disney's Hollywood Studios: Get a bus from near the park entrance directly to Magic Kingdom Park.

From Disney's Animal Kingdom: Get a bus from near the park entrance directly to Magic Kingdom.

From Disney resorts: Get a bus to Magic Kingdom. Exceptions: the Polynesian Village Resort, Contemporary and Grand Floridian provide Monorail and boat access only. The Contemporary is a 5-minute walk to Magic Kingdom. Fort Wilderness resort provides boat access only. Wilderness Lodge resort provides boat access and buses to Magic Kingdom.

To Epcot:
From Magic Kingdom Park: Get the Express Monorail (faster) or Resort Monorail (slower) to the TTC. Then, change to the Epcot Monorail.

From Disney's Hollywood Studios: Exit via the main entrance and catch a boat to the World Showcase entrance at Epcot. There is also a bus to Epcot's main entrance, which is usually much quicker.

From Disney's Animal Kingdom: Get a bus from the park entrance.

From Disney resorts: Buses from all hotels, except: the Boardwalk, Yacht Club, Beach Club, Swan and Dolphin hotels. At these hotels, there are boats to Epcot's World Showcase entrance.

To Hollywood Studios:
From Magic Kingdom Park and Disney's Animal Kingdom: Get a bus from the front of the park.

From Epcot: Exit via the World Showcase entrance; on the left there is a boat service. Alternatively, exit via the main entrance and catch a bus – this is quicker.

From Disney resorts: All hotels provide a bus service to the park, except: the Boardwalk, Yacht Club, Beach Club, Swan and Dolphin hotels. At these hotels, there are boats to the main park entrance.

To Disney's Animal Kingdom: Direct buses from all resorts and other theme parks.

To Disney Springs:
From Disney Resorts: There are buses from all hotels. From Old Key West there are boats and buses. From Port Orleans (both French Quarter and Riverside) there are the boats and buses. From Saratoga Springs and the Treehouse Villas, there are boats and buses to Disney Springs. There is also a bridge from Saratoga Springs to Disney Springs.

From the theme parks: There are no direct buses from theme parks to Disney Springs before 4:00pm. Before 4:00pm, you must first go to a Disney resort and get a bus from there to Disney Springs.

From Blizzard Beach: Go to any hotel and then catch a Disney Springs bus.

To Blizzard Beach:
From the theme parks and Disney resorts: Take a bus to Animal Kingdom Park and then get a Blizzard Beach shuttle bus from Animal Kingdom Park.

From Disney Springs: Get a bus to any Disney resort. Take a bus to Animal Kingdom Park and then get a Blizzard Beach shuttle bus from Animal Kingdom Park.

To Typhoon Lagoon:
From the theme parks and Disney resorts: Go to any resort hotel and catch a Disney Springs bus. At Disney Springs, there is a shuttle to Typhoon Lagoon.

From Disney Springs: Catch the direct shuttle bus to Typhoon Lagoon.

To ESPN Wide World of Sports: Buses from the All-Star Resorts, Caribbean Beach Resort and Pop Century only. From other resorts, you will need to reach one of the aforementioned resorts first – this will involve getting a bus to any theme park, then to one of these resorts, and then a third bus to ESPN. If you are considering this, we recommend driving, or getting a taxi, due to the long transfer time involved.

Transportation Hours:
Buses within Walt Disney World operate every 15 to 30 minutes – with a typical interval of 20 minutes. At park closing, buses run every 5 to 10 minutes.

Service from the resorts begins 1 hour prior to park opening. Buses run return trips to resorts until the parks are clear of guests.

Disney has live bus arrival screens at resort bus stops and in the MyDisneyExperience app – here you can see at a glance the estimated arrival times of the next buses. We find these to be accurate.

Buses between parks begin 1 hour prior to the later park opening, and buses run until the later closing park is clear of all guests.

Bus service to and from Disney Springs is available from resort hotels. The last bus back to resorts leaves Disney Springs at 2:00am.

The Magic Kingdom Park monorail beams operate from 1 hour before earliest park opening until one hour after latest park closing. The Epcot beam of the monorail operates from 8:00am to 11:00pm, or until 1 hour after Magic Kingdom closes (whichever is earliest).

Ferries between Magic Kingdom and the TTC, and boats from resorts to Magic Kingdom, begin 30 minutes before park opening including Extra Magic Hours and run until 90 minutes after park closing.

Old Key West and Saratoga Springs resorts run an hourly boat service to Disney Springs from 11:00am to 4:00pm. From 4:00pm onwards this service runs every 30 minutes. The last boat leaves Old Key West at 11:00pm and from Disney Springs at 11:00pm.

OTHER TRANSPORTATION:

Taxis/Uber/Lyft - The Disney bus service is good, but long waits and indirect routes with transfers waste time. You may wish to use a taxi or app-based services Uber and Lyft. These are quicker than the Disney buses and usually cost $10-$15 for a single trip. We do not suggest these services for Magic Kingdom as they drop you off at the TTC, where you need a monorail or ferry transfer to the park. Disney buses drop off at Magic Kingdom itself.
Minnie Van Service - This service is run by Disney via the Lyft app. Drivers are Disney Cast Members and the service runs like Uber but with large SUVs seating 6 people. Rides are more expensive (in the $25-$40 range). These vans also CAN drop you off at Magic Kingdom's entrance unlike the other services above.
Disney Skyliner - This is a brand new ski-style gondola system which will run between Art of Animation/Pop Century, Disney's Caribbean Beach, Disney's Riviera Resort, Disney's Hollywood Studios and Epcot's World Showcase entrance. Guests may have to change gondola en-route. We expect this system will replace buses most of the time (except during lightning) and to be complimentary for hotel guests. Disney has not announced the Skyliner will begin operation in Fall 2019 - the system will not have air conditioning.

Chapter Five | Hotels

Hotels

Having a place to relax after a long day in the parks is essential during a Walt Disney World Resort visit. Thankfully, there are many accommodation options including official Disney-operated hotels and even villas. These serve a wide range of budgets right in the heart of the magic.

There are also partner hotels located on Walt Disney World Resort property, but not run by Disney itself, and then there are hundreds of nearby hotels off-property. Central Florida is a hugely competitive market meaning some world-class luxury hotels are available, as well as many mid-range and budget options.

The on-site hotels are split into four categories:
- **Value** - All Star Resorts (Music, Movies and Sport), Art of Animation, Pop Century and The Campsites at Fort Wilderness Resort
- **Moderate** - Caribbean Beach, Port Orleans (French Quarter and Riverside), Coronado Springs and The Cabins at Fort Wilderness Resort
- **Deluxe** - Animal Kingdom Lodge, Beach Club, BoardWalk Inn, Contemporary Resort, Grand Floridian Resort & Spa, Polynesian Village Resort, Wilderness Lodge, and Yacht Club.
- **Deluxe Villa** - Bay Lake Tower at Disney's Contemporary Resort, Boulder Ridge Villas at Wilderness Lodge, Animal Kingdom Villas (Jambo House and Kidani Village), Beach Club Villas, BoardWalk Villas, Old Key West Resort, Polynesian Villas & Bungalows, Saratoga Springs Resort & Spa, and The Villas at Disney's Grand Floridian Resort & Spa. Disney's Riviera Resort was in construction at the time of writing and is rumored to open in Fall/Winter 2019.

Generally speaking, the more expensive hotels have more elaborate theming, more amenities and more transportation options.

We highly recommend an on-site hotel for a Walt Disney World stay if you can justify the cost. Over the next few pages, you will discover all the extra advantages to staying on-site.

Disney Resort Hotels

The Walt Disney World Resort offers thirty Disney owned resorts on property, covering all price ranges, including Value, Moderate and Deluxe rooms, as well as Deluxe Villas. All are beautifully themed environments and offer distinct advantages over other non-Disney hotels.

Disney Hotel Features and Amenities:

- **MagicBands** with your room key, park tickets, meal vouchers, PhotoPass and more on a wearable bracelet.
- **Laundry facilities** for $3 per load; dryers are $3 a load. Detergent is $1 per load.
- **In-room babysitting services** are available from $18 per hour at all resorts. The Dolphin Resort and Contemporary Resort also offer paid Children's Activity Centers and activities.
- **Entertainment at your hotel** - all hotels have an arcade and host outdoor nightly Disney movie screenings. Other activities at select Disney hotels include basketball, bike and boat rentals, carriage rides, golf courses, archery, fishing, golf cart rentals, jogging paths, gyms, pony rides, tennis courts and volleyball courts.
- **Late checkout** (subject to availability) at no extra cost.
- **Local calls** are 75 cents; there is no charge for calls to Walt Disney World locations.
- **No charge for children under 17** staying in the same room as adults. In rooms with more than two adults, extra adults pay a supplement of $15 to $35 each per night.
- **A Disney shop** in each resort selling merchandise and basic items such as sunscreen.
- **Room occupancy** at Disney hotels is usually four people.
- **A 24-hour front desk**.
- **Overnight self-parking** costs $13 at Value resorts, $19 at Moderates and $24 at Deluxes, per night.
- **Room service** in all rooms for a $3 delivery fee plus 18% gratuity.
- **At least one ATM** per resort.
- **Check in** is at 3:00pm and check out is at 11:00am for all resorts unless stated.
- **All Disney resorts are non-smoking** except in designated areas.
- **Room amenities** include cable TV, coffee and coffee-making facilities, a telephone, a table with two chairs, and an in-room safe. An iron and ironing board are either in rooms or available at the front desk. Most standard rooms have two double beds or one king-size bed.
- **Special rates** for annual passholders, guests with a Disney Visa card and Florida Residents - up to 40% off.
- **Room prices** vary seasonally. Prices listed herein are per night for a standard room with two adults sharing, and include tax at 12.5% (unless stated) and exclude special offers.

Exclusive Disney Hotel Advantages:

- **Complimentary transportation** to all the theme parks, using buses, monorails and boats.
- **Extra Magic Hours**, allowing one hour's early entry into one theme park per day, and to stay up to two hours after park closing at another park.
- **Free parking** at the theme parks and water parks with your MagicBand.
- **Friendly and knowledgeable** Disney Cast Members
- **Free round-trip Magical Express transportation** to and from Orlando International Airport.
- **Complimentary in-room Wi-Fi** and at most public areas at resorts.
- **At least one pool per hotel**.
- **Disney Dining Plans** available with package bookings – savings of up to 40% on meals.
- **A small refrigerator** in every room.
- **A refillable mug program** ($18.99) with unlimited drink refills at resort hotels for your stay.
- **Resort Airline Check In** – Check in for flights directly from your resort, including checking in luggage and receive a boarding card. Available for both domestic and international passengers flying with: Alaska, American, Delta (domestic only), JetBlue, Southwest and United.

All Star Resorts

This 5840-room value resort is actually three separate hotels located next to each other: All Star Music, All Star Sports and All Star Movies. Each resort has giant sculptures and characters appropriate to the theme.

The All-Star resorts are the cheapest resorts in all of Walt Disney World, and because of this you will find that the hotel is often booked by large groups such as cheerleading teams.

Note that there are no Table Service restaurants at any of these hotels. You only have food-court options.

Themeing at these hotels is suited for younger members of the family who will likely enjoy seeing big Disney character icons around the resort. The themeing will not, however, transport you to a different place in the way that some of the more premium resorts do.

Overall, these resorts offer a great value stay for guests on a limited budget and who spend most of their time in the parks.

All-Star Movies - Houses five distinct movie-themed buildings including one themed to 101 Dalmatians and another to Toy Story. Rooms have movie-themed touches. There are two pools. This is the most well-themed of the three All-Star resorts, in our opinion.

All-Star Sports - This was the first value resort at Walt Disney World. There are three pools at this resort, an arcade with video games at Stadium Hall. McDonalds is a 5-minute walk from the resort entrance.

All-Star Music – As well as standard rooms, at this resort there are family suites of 520ft^2 available for up to 6 people. There are two bedrooms and bathrooms in suites, with two 27" TVs, a pullout sofa, a microwave and a fridge.

Location: Animal Kingdom resort area.

> **DINING:**
> **End Zone (Sports)** – Quick Service, Disney Dining Plan accepted, entrées are $9-$17. Open from 6:00am to midnight.
> **Grandstand Spirits (Sports)** – Pool Bar, Disney Dining Plan not accepted. Open from midday to midnight.
> **Intermission (Music)** – Quick Service, Disney Dining Plan accepted, entrées are $6-$14. Open from 6:00am to midnight.
> **Singing Spirits (Music)** – Pool Bar, Disney Dining Plan not accepted. Open from 1:00pm to midnight.
> **World Premiere (Movies)** – Quick Service, Disney Dining Plan accepted, entrées are $8-$14. Open from 6:00am to midnight.
> **Silver Screen Spirits (Movies)** – Pool Bar, Disney Dining Plan not accepted. Open from 1:00pm to midnight.

Theme: Movies, Music and Sports.
Transport: Buses to all Walt Disney World locations – 10 to 15 minutes to Animal Kingdom Park, Epcot and Disney's Hollywood Studios, and 20 minutes to the water parks and Magic Kingdom.
Room size: 260 ft^2.
Room prices: $112-$217 for a standard room, $277-$497 at the All Star Music family suites
Activities: Poolside movies and activities, and an arcade at each of the three resorts.

Hotels

Pop Century Resort

This 2880-room Value resort is a step up from the All Star Resorts on the previous page. It is themed around the second half of the 20th-century.

DINING:
Everything Pop – Quick Service and Snacks, Disney Dining Plan accepted, entrées are $9.50-$15. Open from 6:00am to midnight.
Petals – Pool Bar serving alcoholic and non-alcoholic drinks, Disney Dining Plan not accepted, drinks are $3.80-$12.50.

A step up from the All Star Resorts, Pop Century provides many of the same amenities as the other value resorts.

However, Pop Century Resort opened its doors in late 2003, making it newer than the All Stars (which opened between 1994 and 1999), but older than Art of Animation resort.

Given the slight increase in price we think this is worth the few extra dollars. At certain times of the year, you may find that this resort is actually cheaper than the All Star Resorts.

As well as the Everything Pop food court at this resort, guests are a short walk away from Disney's Art of Animation Resort which has an even greater variety of food options.

At the moment, regular buses connect this resort to all the theme parks. However, once the Disney Skyliner opens (see page 9 for more information - expected in Fall 2019), guests at this resort will have direct gondola access to Disney's Hollywood Studios and Epcot, providing an even more efficient way to reach these theme parks. There may well be an increase in room prices once this resort opens.
Location: Near ESPN Wide World of Sports; connected to Art of Animation resort.
Theme: Pop culture in the second half of the 20th century. Expect to see giant play doh sets, Disney characters, bowling pins, keyboards, 8 track tapes and much more.
Transport: Buses to all locations. Skyliner transportation (see page 9) upon project completion.
Room size: 260 ft^2.
Room prices: $130 to $245 for a standard room
Activities: There are three pools, a playground, an arcade and a "pop jet playground" where jets of water shoot out of the ground.
Extras: There is a 5000-square foot store in the resort.

Art of Animation

This value resort is the newest on property and has its own dedicated bus service. There are four different themed sections at this resort.

Art of Animation is the gold standard for the Value resorts. It is the newest full resort on property, having opened in May 2012.

The theming and atmosphere at Art of Animation is vastly superior to the other Value resorts and is among some of the best on property; the food court is also one of the best on all of Disney property as it features a wide variety of choices.

Rooms at this resort are more expensive than both All Star and Pop Century Resorts, and the majority of rooms here are actually family suites.

Standard rooms at this resort are very popular and it is worth booking far in advance in order to secure them, as suites are significantly more expensive.

Location: Near ESPN Wide World of Sports, connected to Pop Century resort.
Theme: The resort is split up into four sections themed around Disney and Pixar classics. The Little Mermaid area offers standard rooms. Suites are available in the areas themed to Finding Nemo, Cars and The Lion King.
Transport: Buses to all locations on property. Skyliner transportation (see page 9) upon project completion.
Number of rooms: 864 standard rooms, 1120 family suites.
Room size: 260 ft^2 in a standard room and 565 ft^2 in a suite.
Room prices: Standard rooms are priced between $153 and $271; suites are priced between $366 and $613.
Activities: Poolside activities, underwater speakers in main pool and an arcade.
Extras: The suites feature kitchenettes with a table, a master bedroom and three different sleeping spaces.

> **DINING:**
> **Landscape of Flavors Food Court** – Quick Service and Snacks, Disney Dining Plan accepted, entrées are $7-$14.

Port Orleans

Port Orleans is split into two resorts - Riverside (2048 rooms) and French Quarter (1000 rooms). This is a moderate resort with larger rooms than Value resorts.

Port Orleans is our favorite moderate resort: it has fantastic immersive theming, and plenty of amenities available to guests. What's more, guests can use the amenities of both Riverside and French Quarter resorts.

The centerpiece of this resort is the Sassagoula River that flows towards the Disney Springs area.

The resort is also just a short boat ride away from the dining and shopping options at Disney Springs.

Location: Disney Springs resort area.
Transport: Buses to all locations, as well as additional boats to Disney Springs.

Room size: 314 ft^2 for standard rooms.
Room prices: $232 to $350 for a standard room.
Riverside Activities: Five pools, a spa and a kids' pool. There is also an evening carriage ride available. Catch-and-release pole fishing activities are also available for $6 for 30 minutes. There is also a 2-hour fishing excursion priced from $235 to $270 for 5 people.
French Quarter Activities: A dragon water slide, a games room and a water playground by the pool. The pool is heated and has a Jacuzzi. Bike rentals are available.
Extras: Some rooms also contain a trundle bed.

DINING:
Mardi Grogs (French Quarter) – Pool Bar, Disney Dining Plan not accepted, drinks are $4.50-$17. Open from 11:30am to 9:45pm.
Scat Cat's Club (French Quarter) – Drinks lounge, Disney Dining Plan not accepted. Open 4:00pm to midnight.
Sassagoula Floatworks and Food Factory (French Quarter) – Snacks and Quick Service, Disney Dining Plan accepted, entrées are $6-$18. Open from 6:00am to midnight.
Boatwright's Dining Hall (Riverside) – Table Service, Disney Dining Plan accepted, entrées are $19-$35. Open from 5:00pm to 10:00pm.
Muddy Rivers (Riverside) – Pool Bar, No Disney Dining Plan, drinks are $5.50-$8.50. Open 11:30am to 9:30pm.
River Roost (Riverside) – Drinks lounge, No Disney Dining Plan. Open 4:00pm to 11:30pm.
Riverside Mill – Snacks and Quick Service, Disney Dining Plan accepted, entrées are $6-$16. Open from 6:00am to midnight.

Hotels

Coronado Springs Resort

This 1967-room moderate resort is themed to the Southwest of the US with Mexican influences. This large resort is popular with convention attendees.

Coronado Springs is a large resort and the only moderate-level resort to include a fitness center.

The centerpiece of the resort is a lake, surrounded by beaches with hammocks. The pool here is also our favorite moderate-level pool.

One aspect to bare in mind is that the resort is spread out meaning that it can take a while from your room to a food location or the hotel reception. An internal resort golf-cart shuttle system takes you between area (villages).

Location: Animal Kingdom resort area.
Transport: Buses to all Walt Disney World locations. Disney's Hollywood Studios, Animal Kingdom Park and Epcot are a 10-minute bus ride, and Blizzard Beach is just 5 minutes away. The furthest park is Magic Kingdom which is 20 minutes away by bus.
Room size: 314 ft^2.
Room prices: Between $208 and $331 per night for a standard room.
Activities: Towering above the main pool is a Mayan pyramid and water slide, with an archaeological site for the kids too. This resort is huge and surrey bike rentals are available. Every Wednesday, there is a *Viva Coronado Springs Fiesta* where guests can taste Mexican treats and take part in special recreational activities.
Extras: There is an air-conditioned 400-seat open-air-style market food court.

Dining:
Maya Grill – Table Service, Disney Dining Plan accepted, entrées are $19-$58. Open from 7:00am to 10:00pm.
Pepper Market Food Court – Quick Service, Disney Dining Plan accepted, entrées are $6-$16. Open from 7:00am to 11:00pm.
Rix Café – Quick Service, Disney Dining Plan accepted, entrées are $7-$10.50. Open from 6:30am to 11:00pm.
Rix Sports Bar and Grill – Drinks Lounge and Meals, Disney Dining Plan accepted, entrées are $10 to $28. Open from 5:00pm to 2:00am.
Siestas Cantina – Quick Service and Bar, Disney Dining Plan accepted, entrées are $10 to $12.
The Laguna Bar – Bar, Disney Dining Plan accepted, entrées $6-$8.

There are 3 other restaurants and room service. There are arcades, bars, playgrounds and pools. The rooms are located in three villages around "Lago Dorado". This resort contains a convention center.

Hotels

Caribbean Beach Resort

This 2112-room moderate resort is themed to the Caribbean with some of the largest rooms in this price category.

This is one of the most relaxing resorts in our opinion and also one of the largest. There is a 45-acre lake in the middle of the resort with paths leading to each building.

This resort is quite big and it can be a 15-minute walk or longer from Centertown (the hub of the resort with dining locations) to your room. This is great for a peaceful ambiance, but can be annoying at the end of a long day in the parks. For this reason, you may wish to consider an upgraded room closer to the resort hub. This is the only moderate resort to offer an option of rooms which sleep 5 people.

Location: Near Epcot, Disney's Hollywood Studios and the Disney Springs area.
Transport: Buses to all locations. Skyliner transportation (see page 9) upon project completion.
Number of rooms: 2112 rooms in 33 buildings, grouped into 6 villages.
Room size: 340 ft^2.
Room prices: $194 to $322 per night for a standard room. Pirate themed rooms cost $267 to $378 per night.
Activities: The Centertown area has food courts, restaurants, shops, arcades, pools and a water slide. There are bike and boat rentals too. There are four pools at this resort. Hammocks are available at no charge by the lake.
Extras: Pirate themed rooms are available at a surcharge. A two-hour Caribbean Pirate Adventure Cruise is available for kids ages 4-12 for $39 to $49.

Dining:
Banana Cabana – Pool Bar, Disney Dining Plan not accepted. Open from midday to midnight.
Centertown Market – Quick Service, Disney Dining Plan accepted, entrées are $7-$14.50. Open from 6:00am to 11:30am and 5:00pm to 11:00pm.
Sebastian's Bistro – Table Service, Disney Dining Plan accepted, entrées are $14-$34. Open from 11:00am to 10:00pm.
Spyglass Grill – Quick Service, Disney Dining Plan accepted, entrées are $7-$14. Open from 7:00am to 10:00pm.

Coming Soon:
Disney Riviera Resort is currently under construction and is expected to open in late 2019. Details are very limited at the moment - at the time of writing we do not even have confirmation of whether this is a moderate or a deluxe-level resort. We do know that there will be a rooftop restaurant with views of both Disney's Hollywood Studios' and Epcot's nighttime spectaculars, and that there will be about 300 rooms in total. The resort will likely be a sister resort to Caribbean Beach resort and may also share some amenities, although this has not yet been confirmed. Disney Riviera Resort will include access to the Skyliner transportation system when that opens (see page 9).

Yacht Club Resort

This is the first of the deluxe-level resorts we will look at it. The Yacht Club is a 630-room resort located next to Epcot's World Showcase entrance on Crescent Lake.

The Yacht Club is one of our favourite resorts on all of Walt Disney World property.

The resort's location is within walking distance of Epcot, and a boat ride away from Disney's Hollywood Studios.

The 3.5-million liter pool is by far the best at Walt Disney World and is shared with the Beach Club Resort - the pool even has a sand bottom.

The Yacht Club feels like true a deluxe resort throughout and comes highly recommended.

Transport: Epcot is a 5-minute walk, or you can catch the boat from the dock at the back of the hotel. Hollywood Studios is a 20-minute boat ride, or a similar walk. You can reach Magic Kingdom Park, Animal Kingdom, the Disney water parks and Disney Springs by bus.

Room size: 380 ft^2

Room prices: Standard rooms cost between $456 and $749 per night.

Activities: The best pool at Walt Disney World, with water jets, a water slide, a hot tub and a quiet pool. Fantasia Gardens mini-golf is located close by. There is also a volleyball court, a health club, jogging paths and an arcade.

Extras: This hotel also features a clothes store and an in-house barber.

DINING:

Ale and Compass – Table Service, Disney Dining Plan accepted, entrées are $17-$36. Open from 6:30am to 11:00pm.

Ale and Compass Lounge – Lounge, serves Breakfast, Disney Dining Plan accepted for breakfast food items only. Open from 6:00am to midnight.

Beaches and Cream – Table Service, Disney Dining Plan accepted, entrées are $9-$16. Desserts are the specialty here including the famous 'kitchen sink'. Open from 11:00am to 11:00pm.

Crew's Cup Lounge – Drinks Lounge, Disney Dining Plan not accepted. Open from midday to midnight. Serve snacks.

Hurricane Hanna's Grille – Quick Service, Disney Dining Plan accepted, entrées are $10-$13. Open from 11:00am to 6:00pm.

Yachtsman Steakhouse – Signature Table Service Restaurant, Disney Dining Plan accepted (2 credits per person), entrées are $31-$125. Open from 5:30pm to 10:00pm.

Beach Club Resort

Located next to the Yacht Club, the Beach Club is a 585-room resort by Epcot's World Showcase entrance.

The Beach Club is the sister resort of the Yacht Club and comes equally highly recommended with its amazing pool, beach-side charm and great location.

For larger groups, the Beach Club villas are also available comprising of studios, 1-bed and 2-bed apartments.

Overall, this resort feels slightly less busy that the Yacht Club next door, with fewer non-resident visitors.

Transport: Epcot is a 5-minute walk, or you can catch the boat from the dock at the back of the hotel. Hollywood Studios is a 20-minute boat ride or a 20-minute walk. You can reach Magic Kingdom Park, Animal Kingdom Park, the Disney water parks and Disney Springs by bus.
Room size: 380 ft^2.
Room prices: Standard rooms are priced between $441 and $732 per night. 1 bedroom villas cost $828 to $1285 per night, and 2-bedroom villas are $1721 to $2959 per night.
Activities: The hotel has the best pool at Walt Disney World, with water jets, a water slide, a hot tub and a quiet pool. Fantasia Gardens mini-golf is located close by. There is a volleyball court, a health club, jogging track, an arcade, and tennis courts. There is a scavenger hunt available from Guest Services.
Extras: At Atlantic Wear and Wardrobe Emporium you can buy swimwear and clothes, food, souvenirs and does film processing. Periwig's does haircuts. There are penny and quarter press machines and an ATM machine.

DINING:
Cape May Café – Character Buffet at Breakfast and Non-Character Buffet at Dinner, Disney Dining Plan accepted, $36 per adult and $21 per child at breakfast, $48 per adult and $27 per child at dinner. Open from 7:30am to 9:30pm. Does not serve lunch.
Martha's Vineyard Lounge – Drinks Lounge, Disney Dining Plan not accepted. Open from 5:30pm to midnight. Serves snacks priced between $9 and $13.

Boardwalk Inn Resort

This small 378-room resort is themed to a seaside town's boardwalk. The Boardwalk is an attraction unto itself and is amazingly located by Epcot.

The Boardwalk Inn is a fun resorts with a unique 1920s and 1930s seaside charm theme. As with the two previous resorts, The Boardwalk is located just steps from Epcot.

The Boardwalk Inn is one of Walt Disney World's more intimate resorts due to its small size.

Here as well as standard rooms, there areas studios, 1-bedroom and 2-bedroom apartments which can accommodate larger groups.

Location: Between Epcot and Disney's Hollywood Studios, opposite the Yacht and Beach Club resorts.
Transport: It is a 5-minute walk to Epcot, although a boat service is also available. Disney's Hollywood Studios is a 20-minute walk, or a boat takes the same length of time. Bus transportation is available to the rest of Walt Disney World.
Room size: 390 ft^2.
Room prices: $498 to $786 per night for a standard room. The 1-Bedroom Boardwalk Villas are priced between $694 and $1051 per night, whereas the 2-Bedroom villas go for between $1042 and $1807 per night.
Activities: There is a main pool with swimming tubes as well as two other pools, a health club and a private spa. Bike rentals are available at $7 per hour.

DINING:

AbracadaBar – Lounge, Disney Dining Plan not accepted. Cocktails are $12.50, wines $9 to $21 per glass, and beers are $7-$10
Ample Hills Creamery – Snacks, Disney Dining Plan not accepted. Ice creams $7 to $10.
Big River Grille and Brewing Works – Table Service, Disney Dining Plan accepted, entrées are $912-$27. Open from 11:00am to midnight.
Boardwalk Bakery – Snacks and Quick Service, Disney Dining Plan accepted.
Boardwalk Pizza Window – Quick Service, Disney Dining Plan accepted, pizza slices are $6-$7, whole pizzas are $21-$24. Open from midday to midnight.
Boardwalk To Go – Snacks, Disney Dining Plan not accepted, entrées are $4-$9.
ESPN Club – Table Service, Disney Dining Plan accepted, entrées are $15-$27.
Flying Fish – Signature Restaurant, Disney Dining Plan accepted (2 Table Service credits), entrées are $20 to $48. Dinner only.
Leaping Horse Libations – Quick Service and Bar, Disney Dining Plan accepted, entrées are $8-$12. Open from 11:00am to 6:30pm.
Trattoria al Forno – Table Service, Disney Dining Plan accepted, entrées are $17-$38.

Hotels

Wilderness Lodge Resort

This 728-room deluxe hotel is located just a short boat journey away from Magic Kingdom Park. It immerses you into a turn-of-the-century National Park lodge.

Wilderness Lodge is one of our favourite themed resorts, as it feels like home from the moment you step inside.

Its location is only minutes away from Magic Kingdom Park, yet it feels a world away from its hustle and bustle of the theme parks. The woodland-style setting is the perfect invitation to relax.

Transport: Buses to all parks; there is also a boat service to Magic Kingdom Park and to Fort Wilderness resort.
Room size: 340 ft².
Room prices: Standard rooms are priced between $378 and $669 per night. Deluxe villas are also available with 1-Bedrooms priced between $673 and $1073 per night, and 2-Bedrooms between $1116 and $1935 per night. Studio villas are also available.
Activities: There are several pools, a water slide, two hot tubs, jogging paths, an arcade, boat and bike rentals, flag family, Wonders of The Lodge guided tours and a hidden mickey hunt.
Extras: Concierge rooms are available. Studios, 1-bedroom and 2-bedroom apartments are also available including the Copper Creek Villas which opened in 2017.

DINING:
Artist Point – Signature Table Service, Disney Dining Plan accepted (2 credits per person), entrées are $34-$51. Open from 5:00pm to 9:00pm. The restaurant will move to character dining from November 10, 2018.
Geyser Point Bar and Grill – Snacks and Quick Service, Disney Dining Plan not accepted, entrées are $8-$12.50. Open from 7:00am to midnight.
Roaring Fork – Snacks and Quick Service, Disney Dining Plan accepted, entrées are $9-$14. Open from 6:00am to midnight.
Territory Lounge – Drinks lounge, Disney Dining Plan not accepted. Also serves snacks. Open from 4:30pm to midnight.
Trout Pass Pool Bar – Pool Bar, Disney Dining Plan not accepted.
Whispering Canyon Café – Table Service, Disney Dining Plan accepted, entrées are $14 to $24 at lunch. Dinner offers a la carte options priced at $23-$35 or a 'All-You-Care-To-Enjoy Skillet' for $33. Open from 7:30am to 10:00pm.

Hotels

Animal Kingdom Lodge Resort

This 1293-room African-themed resort extends the magic of Disney's Animal Kingdom Park with animals roaming the savanna just outside your window .

Animal Kingdom Lodge Resort is a magical place to stay at and is the closest thing you will get to experiencing a night in Africa while in sunny Florida.

The resort features three different savannas, each with unique animals and a distinct look and feel.

Although, all rooms have balconies at this resort, it should be noted that this does not mean they all have views of the savannas and animals - those views cost at least $170 more than standard rooms.

You are welcome to explore all the savannas during your stay. A guide detailing where to find different species is available in all guest rooms.

Many guests worry that the smells from the animals will reach the rooms, but this is not the case. Rooms are also soundproofed to keep out the animal noise.

Transport: Buses to all locations. An internal shuttle service operates.
Room size: 344 ft².
Room prices: $389 to $622 per night in a standard room. Jambo House and Kidani Village villas are priced at $1143 to $1855 each night for a 1-bedroom, and $1838 to $3094 for a 2-bedroom.
Activities: There are many pools and a fitness center.
Extras: There are savannah safari options for an extra charge.

DINING:
Boma – Breakfast and dinner buffet, $24 per adult and $14 per child at breakfast, Disney Dining Plan accepted, $43 per adult and $24 per child at dinner. Open from 7:30am to 11:00am and 4:30pm to 9:30pm. Does not serve lunch.
Dine with an Animal Specialist – Lunch at Sanaa and learn about the resort's animals from an animal keeper during your meal. Diners get a table facing the Sunset Savannah. Offered Wednesday and Saturday at 11:00am. The cost is $60 per adult and $35 per child, including a gratuity. Reserve on 407-938-4755.
Jiko: The Cooking Place – Signature Restaurant, Disney Dining Plan accepted (2 table service credits), entrées are $34-$49. Open from 5:30pm to 10:00pm.
Sanaa – Table Service, Disney Dining Plan accepted, entrées are $8-$22 at breakfast and lunch, and $19-$34 at dinner. Open 7:00am to 9:00pm.
The Mara – Snacks and Quick Service, Disney Dining Plan accepted, entrées are $3-$11.
Uzima Springs Pool Bar – Pool bar, Disney Dining Plan not accepted.
Victoria Falls – Lounge, Disney Dining Plan not accepted. Serves drinks and snacks.

Hotels

Grand Floridian Resort & Spa

The height of sophistication, the Victorian-themed Grand Floridian remains unmatched in splendor. This 900-room deluxe hotel offers a huge range of dining options to Guests.

"Pure opulence" is perhaps the best way to describe the Grand Floridian resort. From the moment you step into the lobby, you are transported to a different era as you smell the hotel's unique aroma and hear a live piano music playing.

The resort's grounds are romantic, yet relaxed and a pathway connects the resort with the Polynesian Village Resort next door. The hotel of course has its own private pool.

The hotel is, however, a little more "stuffy" (but in no way snobby) and less fun than some of the other resorts, in our opinion. If you like "being waited on hand and foot", there is no better choice.

The standard rooms are also among the largest at the Walt Disney World resort, measuring 440 ft².

Guests should be aware that the cheapest rooms at the resort are not located in the main building and will require a walk outdoors without shelter. This is atmost a 3-minute walk but is something to bear in mind in case of inclement weather. These outer buildings are exceptionally peaceful, so this may be a benefit to some Guests.

Magic Kingdom Park is only a short monorail or boat ride away, and there is are fantastic views of Cinderella Castle from across the resort.

The on-site "Senses" spa offers facials, massages, body therapies, nails, kids services and full spa packages.

The resort's wealth of eateries here means that the entirety of the next page is dedicated to your dining options here.

Location: One stop away from Magic Kingdom Park on the monorail.
Transport: Monorail to Magic Kingdom Park, the Contemporary Resort, the Transportation and Ticketing Center (TTC), Epcot and the Polynesian Village Resort. For Epcot you should change monorail lines at the TTC.
Room prices: Standard room pricing varies between $664 and $957. 1-Bedroom Villas are priced at $1448 to $2529, with 2-Bedroom Villas priced at $2356 to $3673 per night. Standard rooms sleep 5 people and Dormer rooms sleep 4 people.
Activities: Arts and crafts, story time, afternoon tea, Floridian Express guided tour for $15, princess promenade with Cinderella, character dinners, silhouette cut-outs for $15 to $24, two pools – one with a water slide and a water play area, electrical water pageant viewing, tennis courts, boats

available for rental (extra charge), jogging, volleyball, spa and complimentary 24-hour health club, croquet and more.

Extras: Valet parking is available for $33 plus a tip. There are six shops in the main building. The Villas at Grand Floridian are also available to stay at: accommodation includes studios, 1-bedroom and 2-bedroom apartments (sleeping up to 8 people).

DINING:

1900 Park Fare – Character Buffet, Disney Dining Plan accepted, Breakfast – adults $35, children $20, Dinner – adults $45, children $27. Open from 8:00am to 8:20pm. Does not serve lunch.
Beach Pool Bar – Pool Bar with Quick Service options, serves entrées priced at $10-$16 and drinks, Disney Dining Plan accepted. Open from 11:00am to 7:00pm.
Citricos – Signature Table Service, Disney Dining Plan accepted (2 Table Service credits), entrées are $30-$49. Open from 5:30pm to 10:00pm.
Courtyard Pool Bar – Pool Bar with Snack options, serves snacks priced at $6-$11 and drinks, Disney Dining Plan not accepted.
Garden View Tea Room – Afternoon Tea, Disney Dining Plan not accepted, tea meals are $35-$50 for adults with a deluxe sharing tea at $150 for 2 people, a children's tea meal is priced at $23. Open from 2:00pm to 5:00pm.
Gasparilla Grill and Games – Snacks and Quick Service, Disney Dining Plan accepted, entrées are $7-$14. Open from 6:00am to 11:30pm.
Grand Floridian Café – Table Service, Disney Dining Plan accepted, entrées are $11-$23 at brunch and $16-$32 at dinner. Open from 7:00am to 9:00pm.
Mizner's Lounge – Drinks Lounge, Disney Dining Plan not accepted. Open from 5:00pm to midnight.
Narcoossee's – Signature Table Service, Disney Dining Plan accepted (2 Table Service credits), entrées are $39-$72. Open from 5:30pm to 10:00pm.
Perfectly Princess Tea Party – Character lunch, Disney Dining Plan not accepted, $334 for one adult and one child, $235 per additional child and $99 per additional adult. Price includes tea for two, decorated cakes and a meet and greet with Sleeping Beauty, as well as other entertainment. Gifts are given to each child, including crowns, a soft toy and certificates. Offered for ages 4 to 12, mainly targeted at girls though boys are welcome and will receive different gifts. The Tea Party takes place from 10:30am to midday daily except Tuesdays and Thursdays.
Victoria and Albert's (Main Dining Room) – Signature Dining, Disney Dining Plan not accepted. A 7-course Menu Prix Fixe is $185 per guest plus $65 for optional wine pairings, plus tax and gratuity. A 10-course menu is priced at $235 per guest ($340 with wine pairings). Open from 5:00pm to 9:45pm.
Victoria and Albert's Queen Victoria Room – Signature Dining, Disney Dining Plan not accepted. Prix Fixe menu at $235 for 10 courses, and an extra $150 when paired with wine.
Victoria and Albert's Chef's Table – Signature Dining, 9 to 10 course meal inside the Kitchen at Victoria and Albert's, Disney Dining Plan not accepted. Pricing is $250 per person without wine or $105 extra with wine pairings, plus tax and gratuity. Takes place at 6:00pm.
Wonderland Tea Party at 1900 Park Fare – Character lunch, cupcakes and tea, Disney Dining Plan not accepted, pricing is $49 per person. Tea Part held from 1:30pm to 2:30pm.

Polynesian Village Resort

With its Hawaiian theme, and amazing location opposite Magic Kingdom Park, the 847-room Polynesian Village is our favorite deluxe resort.

The Polynesian Village Resort is by far our favorite resort across all of the Walt Disney World resort.

The resort's Hawaiian theme is truly relaxing from the amazing background music played throughout the resort to the lobby, every detail counts towards transporting you to a completely different place.

The beach here is one of the resort's best features - it features panoramic views of Cinderella Castle and other nearby Disney resorts. It means in the evenings, you can lay on a hammock or a lounger and watch Magic Kingdom's fireworks from your own resort.

While you cannot go into the lake, you can certainly go inside the volcano-themed pool, which is just a short walk away.

You can also watch a torch lighting ceremony, enjoy the Electrical Water Pageant from the beach or take a boat to Magic Kingdom Park. This is what a vacation should be - immersive, luxurious and laid-back.

Transport: Monorail to the Magic Kingdom, Contemporary Resort, Transportation and Ticketing Center (TTC), Epcot and Polynesian Village Resort. For Epcot, change monorails lines at the TTC. Buses serve all other parks. A boat is available to Magic Kingdom Park and the Grand Floridian resort. It is a 5-minute walk to the TTC.
Room size: 409 ft^2.
Room prices: Standard rooms are $552 to $861. Water-front bungalows are $2845 to $4705.
Activities: A beach, water activities, two pools, waterfall and water slide, underwater jets, in-pool seating, jogging path. Boat rentals (extra fee). Use of the Grand Floridian's health club is complimentary. Check out the torch lighting ceremony five times a week, and the amazingly themed Trader Sam's bar.

DINING:
Barefoot Pool Bar – No Disney Dining Plan. Open from 11:00am to 7:00pm.
Captain Cook's Snack Co. – Quick Service, Disney Dining Plan accepted, entrées are $7-$12.50.
Kona Café – Table Service, Disney Dining Plan accepted, entrées are $10-$16 at breakfast and $14-$34 at dinner and lunch. Open 7:30am to 9:45pm.
Kona Island Sushi – Quick Service, No Disney Dining Plan, entrées are $7-$15.
Oasis Bar and Grill – Pool-side Bar and Quick Service, No Disney Dining Plan, entrées are $10-$17.
Ohana – Table Service, Disney Dining Plan accepted, 'family style' dinner, $40-$49 for adults, $24-$28 for children. Open from 3:30pm to 10:00pm.
Ohana's Best Friends Breakfast with Lilo & Stitch – Character Buffet, Disney Dining Plan accepted, $30-$39 for adults, $20-$25 for kids. Held at 7:30am to 12:00pm.
Pineapple Lanai – Serves dole whip ice creams at $5-$11, Disney Dining Plan accepted.
Spirit of Aloha Dinner Show at Luau Cove – Dinner Show, Family Style Feast, Disney Dining Plan accepted (2 Table Service credits), $61-$78 for adults, $34-$48 for kids, tax and tip included. Runs from 5:15pm to 8:00pm.
Tambu Lounge – Drinks, No Disney Dining Plan
Trader Sam's Grog Grotto – Highly themed drinks lounge and snacks, No Disney Dining Plan. Ages 21+ only after 8:00pm.

Contemporary Resort

Located a five-minute walk from Magic Kingdom Park, this 750-room hotel boasts large standard rooms at 436ft², great dining options and an ultra-modern theme.

The Contemporary Resort is a strange one: if you are looking for amazing theming then you will need to look elsewhere, but if you are looking for proximity to Magic Kingdom Park, a deluxe resort and a wide range of amenities, then you need look no further.

Rooms at the resort are large and Guests who will base their stay around Magic Kingdom couldn't stay any closer to the park.

There are also many water recreation options available.

Pixar Play Zone is an immersive children's activity club which runs each evening (6:00pm to 10:30pm) for kids aged 4 to 12, including meeting 'Toy Story' and 'The Incredibles' characters. Pricing is $65 plus tax per child.

Transport: The monorail takes you directly to Magic Kingdom Park – alternatively it is a 5 minute walk. Epcot can be reached by monorail and changing lines at the Transportation and Ticketing Center. Monorail access to the Polynesian Village and Grand Floridian resorts. Wilderness Lodge and Fort Wilderness are a boat ride away. There are bus services to Disney Springs, Animal Kingdom and Disney's Hollywood Studios, and the water parks.

Room prices: Standard rooms are $465 to $728 per night. Rooms in the main resort building cost an extra $100-$200 per night. Bay Lake Tower rooms are $557 to $778 per night for a studio, $810 to $1191 for a 1-Bedroom Villa and $1058 to $2049 for a 2-Bedroom Villa.

Activities: A fitness center, an arcade, basketball, volleyball, golf, and tennis courts.

Extras: The Villas at Bay Lake Tower include studios, 1-bed and 2-bed apartments.

> **DINING:**
> **California Grill** – Signature Restaurant, Disney Dining Plan accepted (2 Table Service credits), entrées are $37-$74. Open from 5:30pm to 10:00pm. Great views of fireworks. Also serves Brunch on Sundays from 10:00am to 1:00pm, priced at $80 per adult (includes 1 cocktail) and $48 per child.
> **Chef Mickey's Buffet** – Character Buffet, Disney Dining Plan accepted, breakfast and brunch are $38-$43 per adult, $20-$25 per child; dinner is $48-$52 per adult, $27-$33 per child. Open from 7:00am to 11:30am for breakfast, 11:30am to 2:30pm for brunch, and from 5:00pm to 9:30pm for dinner.
> **Contempo Café** – Snacks and Quick Service, entrées are $11-$13, Disney Dining Plan accepted.
> **Cove Bar** – Disney Dining Plan accepted for food. Serves sandwiches, wraps and drinks for $5-$11.
> **Outer Rim** – Pool Bar, No Disney Dining Plan. Open from 4:30pm to 10:30pm.
> **Sand Bar** – Pool Bar, Disney Dining Plan accepted for food. Offers Quick Service meals and drinks from $8.50-$11.50.
> **The Wave** – Table Service, Disney Dining Plan accepted, entrées are $12-$20 at breakfast and lunch, and $18-$34 at dinner. Open 7:30am to 10:00pm.

Fort Wilderness Resort & Campground

This resort is split into 788 campsites are in the value range, the 409 cabins are in the moderate category.

Fort Wilderness is a real campground just a boat ride away from Magic Kingdom Park.

The resort is an unapologetically authentic camping experience. It is probably not for you if you want a spa, hotel towels or 24 hour room service.

At the most basic you have a campsite where you can bring your RV and tents and camp out under the stars or in your vehicle. Here you have shared shower and restroom facilities and must provide your own towels and toiletries. If you are the outdoorsy-type this could be perfect.

Alternatively, a big step up are the Wilderness Cabins which are just like many of Disney's hotel rooms but in individual units.

At the resort there are countless outdoor activities and sports and several of our favorite dining experiences are here including the *Hoop Dee Doo Musical Revue* and *Mickey's Backyard BBQ*.

Location: In a forest between Magic Kingdom and Epcot.
Transport: Due to the sheer size of this resort hotel (it is in a 750-acre forest), there is an internal bus system. For Magic Kingdom Park, take the Magic Kingdom boat from the marina. There are buses to the other parks and Disney Springs. You can also rent a golf cart for $59 plus tax per day (we recommend pre-booking these).
Room size: Wilderness Cabins are 504 ft², 12' wide x 42' long. Campsite spaces are 25' wide and vary between 25' and 65' in length.
Room prices: $79 to $202 per night per campsite, $377-$ per night per cabin.
Activities: Horse and pony rides, a petting farm, bike rentals, a 2.3-mile jogging trail, beach volleyball, basketball, shuffleboard, tetherball, and nature walks.

> **DINING:**
> **Hoop-Dee-Doo Musical Revue** – Family style feast with live entertainment, Disney Dining Plan accepted (2 Table Service credits). There are three categories of seating. Adults pay between $64-$72 and children $38-$43. Shows are performed at 4:00pm, 6:15pm and 8:30pm.
> **Meadow Snack Bar** – Snacks and Quick Service, Disney Dining Plan accepted, entrées are $8-$10.50. Open seasonally.
> **Mickey's Backyard BBQ** – Character dinner buffet with live entertainment, Disney Dining Plan accepted (2 Table Service credits), prices are $57 per adult and $33 per child. Open from 6:30pm to 9:30pm. Operates from March to December. Characters do not visit every table but do appear for dancing.
> **Trail's End Restaurant** – Breakfast and Dinner Buffet, Disney Dining Plan accepted, the breakfast buffet is $18-$22 per adult and $10-$12 per child, the weekend brunch menu is $23-$25 per adult and $13-$15 per child, and the dinner buffet is $27-$33 per adult and $16-$19 per child.

Old Key West Resort

Old Key West is in the deluxe villa category, offering a home away from home. The 709-room resort is themed to turn-of-the-century Key West.

Old Key West is the true definition of a resort. You can stay here and spend your vacation at the resort alone and enjoy all its offerings, without needing to set foot in a theme park - it really is a big place.

Accommodations at this DVC resort are among the largest on Walt Disney World property. The resort is also often discounted meaning you can get a great deal here.

The fact it is a large resort with so many amenities may be an inconvenience to guests - especially those using the Disney buses to get around. There are five bus stops within the resort, so be sure to remember which one is closest to your room. For such a large resort it is worth mentioning that food options are quite limited. This is likely because all the accommodations have kitchen facilities. However, Disney Springs is a just short boat ride away and has an abundance of dining options.

Location: Between Epcot and Disney Springs. Next to Disney's Lake Buena Vista golf course.
Transport: Buses to all Walt Disney World destinations. There is also a water ferry to Disney Springs.
Room size: Studio: 376 ft^2, One Bedroom: 942 ft^2, Two Bedrooms: 1,333 ft^2, Grand Villa: 2,022 ft^2.
Room prices: Studio: $395-$590, One Bedroom: $537-$840, Two Bedroom: $746-$1367. Rates for Grand Villas go up to $2000 per night.
Activities: Four pools, a white sand beach, volleyball courts, watercraft rentals, a jogging trail, bike rentals, arcades, basketball courts, shuffleboard, a fitness center, tennis courts, video rentals, air hockey, pool, darts, poolside movies and bingo.
Extras: Ask for a "Hank's

DINING:
Good's Food To Go – Snacks and Quick Service, entrées are $7.50-$10.50, Disney Dining Plan accepted. Open from 7:30am to 10:00pm.
Gurgling Suitcase – Poolside bar and Quick Service, entrées are $8.50-$10.50, Disney Dining Plan accepted. Open from 11:30am to midnight.
Olivia's Café – Table Service, Disney Dining Plan accepted, entrées are $10-$27 at lunch and dinner, and $13-$18 at breakfast. Open from 7:30am to 10:00pm.
Turtle Shack Poolside Snacks – Snacks and Quick Service, Disney Dining Plan accepted, entrées are $8-$10.50. This is also a full service poolside bar.

Happenings" newsletter to take a look at all the fun additional daily offerings that take place throughout the resort.

Saratoga Springs Resort

Saratoga Springs is in the deluxe villa category and in many ways mirrors Old Key West Resort. This 1260-room resort in themed to Saratoga Springs in upstate New York.

Saratoga Springs is very similar to Old Key West, although this resort has slightly smaller rooms.

This resort feels like a home away from home, with amenities meaning that going to the theme parks may not end up being too high on your list - you may just way to stay at "home" and relax.

As the accommodations all have cooking facilities, the dining options are limited. You are, however, just a short boat ride away from Disney Springs where there are countless food options.

The Treehouse villas are unique to this resort: these villas are elevated 10 feet off the ground, offering great surrounding views and allowing you to feel immersed in nature - a truly unique experience.

Location: Disney Springs resort area.

Transport: Buses to all Walt Disney World locations, except Disney Springs where a boat service is available.
Room size:
Studio – 355 ft^2 (up to 4 guests), 1-bedroom – 714 ft^2 (up to 4 guests), 2-bedrooms – 1075 ft^2 (up to 8 guests), 3-bedroom treehouse villas - 1074 ft^2 (up to 9 guests), Grand Villa – 2113 ft^2 (up to 12 guests).
Room prices: Studio – $395-$590, 1-bedroom – $537-$840, 2-bedroom – $764-$1367, 3-bedroom Treehouse villas - $958-$1610. Rates for the Grand Villas go up to about $2000 per night.
Activities: A pool with a water slide, two whirlpools and an interactive children's play area, an arcade, tennis courts and bicycle rentals.
Extras: Senses – a full service spa and health club (book by calling 407-WDW-SPAS).

> **DINING:**
> **On The Rocks** – Pool Bar, Disney Dining Plan not accepted, serves alcoholic and non-alcoholic beverages.
> **The Artist's Palette** – Snacks and Quick Service, Disney Dining Plan accepted, entrées are $9-$14 at lunch and dinner, and $6.50-$11.50 at breakfast. Open from 7:00am to 11:00pm.
> **The Turf Club Grill** – Table Service, Disney Dining Plan accepted, entrées are $18-$36. Open 5:00pm to 10:00m.
> **The Turf Club Lounge** – Bar, Disney Dining Plan not accepted.

On-Site Non-Disney Hotels

There are several hotels that are *not* run by Disney but which *are* on Disney property. The differences between these hotels and Disney hotels are generally the following:

• No Extra Magic Hours (extended theme park hours), with a few exceptions.
• No Disney Dining Plans.
• Complimentary transportation between the hotels and the theme parks, although it runs less often than at Disney's hotels.
• No complimentary Disney Magical Express airport transportation
• Prices are generally lower than at Disney hotels
• Theming is largely non-existent.
• Some hotels charge extra resort fees - we have included these.
• Many of these hotels are part of major chains allowing you to redeem loyalty points.

Unfortunately, there are no advertised room rates for these resorts, so prices listed are average nightly prices for an example trip booked 8 months in advance for June 1-6, 2019 based on 2 adults and 2 children (under 10) in a room.

We would recommend these on-site hotels over off-site hotels due to their location and transportation offerings.

Walt Disney World Swan and Dolphin Resorts

Of all the non-Disney, on-site hotels, these resorts are is the closest to being a fully-fledged Disney resort.

The Swan Resort and Dolphin Resort are sister resorts located just across the water from each other.

Location: Between Epcot and Disney's Hollywood Studios.
Transport: Boats to Disney's Hollywood Studios and Epcot, or a 15-minute walk. Buses to other Walt Disney World locations.
Number of rooms: 756 (swan) and 1509 (dolphin)
Room size: 340 ft^2 (swan) and 360 ft^2 (dolphin)
Room prices: Around $285 including taxes and resort fees.
Activities: Several pools, four whirlpools, boat rentals, volleyball courts, gym and spa.
Extras: Both these hotels offer Extra Magic Hours (extended theme park hours) – a benefit usually only Disney hotel guests get. Suites are available. Wi-Fi is included. Hotel parking is $23 per day, plus tax.

DINING:
Garden Grove (Swan)– Table Service, entrées are $15-$20 at lunch and $30-$37 at dinner. Characters at dinner nightly, and at breakfast on weekends.
Il Mulino (Swan)– Table Service, entrées are $16-$45. Serves dinner only.
Kimonos: Sushi and Rolls (Swan) – Table Service, sushi rolls are $7-$15.50.
Cabana Bar and Grill (Dolphin)– Quick Service, entrées are $13-$19.
Fresh Mediterranean Market (Dolphin) – Breakfast and Lunch. Buffet and a la carte options. $27 for adults and $17 for kids.
Picabu Buffetaria (Dolphin) – Quick Service, entrées are $7.50-$16.
Shula's Steak house (Dolphin) – Table Service, entrées are $28-$105.
The Dolphin Fountain – Quick Service, entrées are $12-$17.
Todd English's Bluezoo (Dolphin) – Table Service, entrées are $29-$60.

Hotels

Doubletree by Hilton Orlando - Disney Springs

Location: Disney Springs area.
Transport: Free shuttle service to Walt Disney World theme parks, water parks and Disney Springs. Can also walk to Disney Springs.
Number of rooms: 229
Room size: Standard room is 350 ft², up to 850 ft² for 2-bed suites.
Room prices: $165 per night.
Activities: Pool, whirlpool, splash pad, tennis court and gym.
Extras: All rooms are suites with bedrooms, plus a separate living area. There is a 5% AAA discount. Parking is $22 per night including tax. Breakfast is included in most rates.

Dining: *Evergreen Café* - Breakfast buffet, lunch and dinner table service. A lounge and pool side bar are also available.

Best Western Lake Buena Vista

Location: Disney Springs area.
Transport: Buses to all Walt Disney World theme parks every 30 minutes. Can walk to Disney Springs.
Number of rooms: 325
Room size: 325-345 ft².
Room prices: $149 per night.
Activities: Heated outdoor pool, children's pool, fitness center and an arcade.
Extras: Free Wi-Fi and self-parking, official Disney souvenir shop, convenience store, laundry facility, transportation to Premium Outlets, complimentary newspapers (Mon-Fri) and a car rental desk. Room service is available. AAA discount is available (about 15%). Breakfast is included in most room rates.

Dining:
Trader's Island Grill – Buffet and Table Service, serves breakfast and dinner.
Flamingo Cove Lounge Marketplace – Convenience store with grab-and-go eating options.

Shades of Green

Location: Magic Kingdom area.
Theme: Upscale Country Club.
Transport: Complimentary transportation to the Disney theme parks. Affordable paid transportation is available to SeaWorld and Universal Orlando.
Number of rooms: 586
Room size: 480 ft².
Room prices: From $119 to $159 per night
Activities: Magnolia Spa, 2 PGA golf courses surround this resort, gym, arcade, two pools, tennis courts and a playground.
Extras: Extra Magic Hours.

This is an exclusive resort for the military and their families and select other service members only – full details are available at shadesofgreen.org/accommodations/eligibility. Upon check-in, a valid military ID or DOD ID, and current Leave and Earnings Statement (LES) are required. Room rates are based on military rank or civilian grade at the time of check-in.

Dining:
Mangino's – Fine dining.
The Garden Gallery – Table Service family restaurant with buffets.
Express Cafe – Quick Service restaurant.
Java Cafe – Serves Starbucks coffee and pastries.
America, The Ice Cream Parlor – 1950s themed ice cream parlor.

Holiday Inn Orlando - Disney Springs

Location: Disney Springs area.
Transport: Complimentary shuttle to Disney Theme Parks every 30 minutes. Typhoon Lagoon, Blizzard Beach & Disney Springs buses run on a scheduled basis.
Number of rooms: 323
Room prices: $185 per night.
Activities: Gym, outdoor pool, games room,
Extras: Self-parking is $14 per night. Wi-Fi in all rooms. Breakfast is usually included in the room price. There are on-site laundry facilities.
Dining:
Palm Breezes Restaurant – A fresh approach to Classic American recipes. Serves Breakfast and Dinner only.
Grab and Go – Quick Service outlet.
Palm Breezes Bar – Bar.

Hilton Orlando Buena Vista Palace Disney Springs

Location: Disney Springs area.
Transport: Complimentary shuttle to Disney Theme Parks every 30 minutes. Typhoon Lagoon, Blizzard Beach & Disney Springs buses run on a scheduled basis.
Number of rooms: 1014
Room size: 400 ft².
Room prices: $265 per night.
Activities: Gym, spa and salon, heated swimming pools, tennis and basketball courts and a treasure hunt.
Extras: In room refrigerator. Suites, room service and babysitting are available. Parking is $18 per day.
Dining:
Citrus 28 - Quick snacks and Starbucks coffee.
Letterpress - Table service restaurant. Buffet breakfast with Disney characters on Sunday.
Shades - Poolside bar with quick bites.
Sunnies - Lobby bar.

Four Seasons Orlando

Location: Golden Oak community/Epcot-Magic Kingdom area.
Transport: Coaches every 30 minutes to Magic Kingdom Park, and every hour to the other 3 theme parks.
Number of rooms: 443 guestrooms (including 68 suites)
Room size: Standard rooms start at 500 ft².
Room prices: $1224 per night.
Activities: Treatments at 'The Spa', a variation of the Bibbidi Bobbidi Boutique called Magical Moments, several pools including a small water park and 11,000 ft² lazy river, 18-hole golf, on-site tennis courts, gym and sauna, and free Kids' Camp.
Extras: Next-day in-room merchandise delivery is available. Wi-Fi is free. Complimentary flavored water and sunscreen are available throughout the resort. There is a late departure lounge with amenities such as Wi-Fi. Valet parking is $30 per night - there is no self-parking available.

Dining:
Ravello Lounge – Bar
Ravello Restaurant – Modern Italian restaurant with character dining breakfast option on Thursdays and Sundays.
PB+G – Casual food
Lickety Split – Dessert and coffee location
Plancha – Cuban American table service location
Capa – Contemporary Spanish steakhouse.

Hotels

Hilton Orlando Lake Buena Vista - Disney Springs

Location: Disney Springs area.
Transport: Complimentary transportation to all the theme parks.
Number of rooms: 814
Room prices: $190 per night.
Activities: 24-hour gym center, two heated outdoor pools including a children's spray pool, and jogging trails.
Extras: Business center, valet parking ($24 per night) and self-parking ($18 per night). The resort fee includes complimentary Wi-Fi and two selected beverages per day, unlimited movie rentals, a coffee maker and a refrigerator. A Disney Character Breakfast is available on Sundays. As well as regular rooms, junior suites and 1 and 2-bedroom suites are also available.

Dining:
24-Hour Main Street Market – Breakfast, lunch and dinner snacks. Serves Starbucks coffee.
Andiamo Italian Bistro – Freshly prepared house specialties.
Benihana Steakhouse and Sushi – Table Service restaurant.
Covington Mill – Serves soups, salads, sandwiches and signature dishes.
John TS – Drinks Lounge. Serves salads, starters, entrées and sandwiches.
Rum Largo Poolside Bar and Café – Bar. Also serves salads, starters and sandwiches.

B Resort & Spa

Location: Disney Springs area.
Transport: Complimentary shuttle to Disney Theme Parks every 30 minutes. Typhoon Lagoon, Blizzard Beach & Disney Springs buses run on a scheduled basis.
Number of rooms: 394
Room prices: $180 per night.
Activities: 24-hour gym, pool with interactive water elements, private cabanas and outdoor fire pits, ice cream parlor and gift shop, kids zone, spa, a hair salon, relaxation lounge, and tennis courts.
Extras: Wi-Fi is available. There are courtesy iPads available at the front desk for guest use. 24 hour in-room dining. Suites. Self-parking is $16 and valet is $21.

Dining:
American Q – Classic American barbeque. The buffet is priced at $35 – a la carte mains are also available.

Pickup – A traditional grab-n-go including an ice cream window service.
Poolside bar and lounge – Drinks lounge.

Off-Site Hotels

The greater Orlando area contains approximately 450 hotels and 115,200 hotel guestrooms.

There are also more than 26,000 vacation home rentals available and more than 20,000 vacation ownership units.

As such, due to the huge number of off-site hotels we cannot cover them in this guide. We prefer to focus on the on-site official and partner hotels.

A popular area to stay is Orlando outside of Disney property is International Drive and its hotels - these hotels are a good mid-point between Walt Disney World and the Universal Orlando resort if you will be visiting both.

Apartment and Villa Rentals:

For the ultimate in space and luxury consider an off-site villa, condo or apartment, especially if you have access to a car. AirBnb.com is a popular site for booking these. Use our exclusive coupon code for $30 off your first booking - visit airbnb.com/c/gdacosta16.

Tickets

There are many ways to access the parks at the Walt Disney World Resort: vouchers, annual passes, buying tickets at the park entrance, online, at a Disney Store and more. To help you decide which option is best for you, this section takes a detailed look at your options.

Understanding Ticket Types

A basic ticket is called a *Base Ticket*. This allows you entry into one park per day. You cannot change parks during the same day. For example, if you wanted to visit Epcot and then go to Magic Kingdom Park on the same day, a base ticket would not allow you to do this.

A *Park Hopper* add-on to your ticket allows entry into all the theme parks, and you can go between them as many times as you want, including visiting multiple parks on the same day.

The *Park Hopper Plus* add-on to your ticket allows you a certain number of entries into Disney's Blizzard Beach water park, Disney's Typhoon Lagoon water park, ESPN Wide World of Sports Complex, a round of mini golf at Fantasia Gardens (before 4:00 pm), a round of mini golf at Winter Summerland (before 4:00 pm), or a round of golf at Oak Trail family walking course.

Buying Tickets at the Gates

If you are having a spontaneous trip and wait until you get to the parks' turnstiles to buy your tickets, you pay the full rate. We recommend booking online before you go - you will save both time and money.

Ticket prices vary depending on a prediction of how busy the parks will be during your stay. The busier the parks, the more expensive tickets are.

Prices of discounted online tickets are on the next page. Tax (of 6.5%) is included.

For tickets of at least 3 days in lenfth, there is a $21.30 discount for tickets bought online versus the gate prices - if you plan to buy at the park gates, add $21.30 to the prices on the next page for tickets over 3 days in length.

Prices were last increased on 16th October 2018.

Note: There are no ticket booths at the Magic Kingdom Park gates; tickets must be bought at Guest Relations at Magic Kingdom Park's entrance, at the Transportation and Ticket Center, from another Disney park's ticket booths, or a Disney hotel.

Florida residents get discounts on gate prices with a Floridian ID when purchasing tickets. These tickets can only be purchased at the Walt Disney World Resort and not in advance.

Online

The official website to purchase your Walt Disney World tickets from is disneyworld.Disney.com. The online pricing can be seen on the next page.

There are also many online ticket resellers who offer tickets at reduced prices. Be sure to buy from a reputable seller.

UnderCoverTourist.com, for example, has up to $65 off some Disney World tickets. We are not able to recommend any companies specifically.

Online Ticket Pricing

	Base Ticket (Adult/Child)	Base Ticket + Park Hopper (Adult/Child)	Base Ticket + Park Hopper Plus (Adult/Child)
1 Day	$116-$137/$111-$132	$175-$196/$169-$190	$201-$223/$196-$217
2 Days	$214-$253/$204-$243	$283-$322/$273-$312	$309-$349/$300-$339
3 Days	$311-$365/$297-$351	$380-$434/$366-$420	$407-$461/$393-$446
4 Days	$395-$462/$377-$444	$475-$541/$457-$524	$502-$568/$484-$550
5 Days	$411-$481/$392-$462	$491-$561/$472-$542	$517-$587/$499-$569
6 Days	$422-$495/$403-$475	$502-$574/$483-$555	$529-$601/$510-$582
7 Days	$432-$507/$413-$487	$512-$587/$492-$567	$539-$613/$519-$594
8 Days	$445-$519/$425-$499	$525-$599/$505-$578	$552-$625/$531-$605
9 Days	$456-$530/$436-$510	$536-$610/$515-$590	$563-$637/$542-$616
10 Days	$465-$539/$444-$518	$545-$619/$523-$598	$571-$646/$550-$625

Prices are seasonal and vary based on the dates of your visit. Prices presented here are for ticket purchased online or when booking a package through Disney including a hotel and tickets - add $21.30 to tickets at least 3 days long if buying at the theme park gates. Prices listed are rounded to the nearest dollar.

You can also buy tickets at any Disney Store for the Walt Disney World Resort at the same prices available at the gate. This will save you time waiting in a queue line on your first day. In the UK, you can only buy "Disney's Ultimate" tickets at the stores.

Disney's Ultimate Tickets - Europe Only

European residents have a few exclusive ticket options available, as many guests who visit Florida stay for 7, 14 or 21 days. Standard tickets cannot accommodate visits of these lengths.

On the official Disney website, a 7-day ticket for 2019 is priced at £399 per adult and £379 per child. A 14-day ticket is £419 and £399. Finally, a 21-day ticket is £439 and £419 respectively. You can often find these tickets cheaper from resellers other than Disney.

Disney's Ultimate Tickets allow you unlimited entry into the theme parks, entertainment complexes, water parks and mini golf courses, and also include photos with Memory Maker.

There are often promotions offering a 14-day ticket for the price of a 7-Day Premium Ticket if staying at a Disney resort.

Ticket Tips

- You will need at least 2 days to tour Magic Kingdom Park, 2 days for Epcot, 1 day for Disney's Hollywood Studios and 1 day for Animal Kingdom. More time allows for a more relaxed pace, which we are sure you will appreciate while on vacation. To see all four parks and their attractions, you will need an absolute minimum of 6 days on your ticket, in our opinion.
- There are free admission shopping, dining and entertainment areas at the Walt Disney World Resort such as Disney Springs and The Boardwalk.
- Check out https://disneyworld.Disney.go.com/special-offers/ for special offers on tickets and hotels, including free tickets and free nights.

Annual Passes

If you are planning on making multiple visits to the Walt Disney World Resort within one year, it can pay to purchase an annual pass.

	Admission to 4 Parks + Free Parking	Park-to-Park Access	Disney Photopass Downloads	No Block-Out Dates	Water Parks Access	Access to Disneyland Resort in California (350 days per year)
Disney Platinum Plus Pass ($1630)	Yes	Yes	Yes	Yes	Yes	Yes
Disney Platinum Pass ($1059)	Yes	Yes	Yes	Yes	Yes	
Disney Platinum Pass ($952)	Yes	Yes	Yes	Yes		

Prices listed above incldue tax. Each pass includes unlimited dailt access to the theme parks, complimentary parking and a MagicBand.

There are additional passes available to Florida Residents and DVC (Disney Vacation Club) members.

Passes also include discounts and offers on dining, merchandise, car rentals, backstage tours, entertainment, sports and recreation (including spa treatments).

Annual passes can be purchased online, on the phone, at park ticket booths or at Guest Services windows at the theme parks.

Chapter Seven | Magic Kingdom Park

Magic Kingdom Park

Disney's Magic Kingdom Park is the most visited theme park in the world with 20.5 million visitors last year. Magic Kingdom Park was the first theme park built at the Walt Disney World Resort and opened on October 1st, 1971.

An important note on Parking:
Guests arriving at *Magic Kingdom Park* by car park at the *Transportation and Ticket Center (TTC)* parking lots. Once parked, you can either catch a tram or follow the pedestrian walkways to the TTC. At the TTC, you should purchase your park entry tickets if you have not done so already.

Then, choose one of two ways to get to the theme park – the Monorail (either the Express line or Resort line) or the Ferryboat. A bus option is also occasionally offered. Within less than 10 minutes, you will be at the entrance to the Magic Kingdom. During peak season, you will have to in a queue line to board the monorail or a ferry here.

The parking lots for all the other theme parks at the Walt Disney World Resort are located by the park entrances, and are thus much easier to navigate.

Parking is charged at the following rates (per day): Cars or Motorbikes - $25. Taxis, Limos, Campers, Trailers, RVs, buses, or Tractor Trailers - $30. Preferred parking is $50.

Disney resort hotel guests can waive the parking fee by scanning their MagicBand at the parking toll plazas. Prices were last raised in October 2018 and are usually raised yearly.

Disney resort guests arriving by complimentary transportation (bus, monorail or boat) will arrive directly at the entrance to Magic Kingdom.

Attraction Key

In the park chapters, we list each attraction individually along with some key information. Here are what the symbols in the next sections mean.

	Does it have Fastpass+?		Minimum height (inches)
	Is there an on-ride photo?		Ride/Show Length
	Average wait time (on peak days)		

Magic Kingdom Park

Main Street, U.S.A.

When you walk into the park, Main Street, U.S.A. is the first thing you will see. Most guests simply refer to this as 'Main Street'.

Main Street, U.S.A. is inspired by Walt Disney's home town of Marceline, Missouri and is themed to recreate a turn-of-the-20th-century street.

Main Street, U.S.A. features shops on both sides of the street and leads to Cinderella Castle at the end. From this 'hub' area in front of the castle, you can venture into one of six themed lands. Due to its location, you will pass Main Street both when entering and exiting the park.

Main Street opens to guests approximately 1 hour before the official park opening time. This means you can enter Main Street and shops and dine before exploring the rest of the park. 5 minutes before the park's scheduled opening time, a show 'Let the Magic Begin' is performed in front of Cinderella Castle to officially open the park.

City Hall is immediately to the left before entering Main Street, U.S.A. This is the one-stop shop for pins, badges, help, disability cards, positive feedback and complaints.

For shopping, the main store here is the huge **Emporium**, but there are many smaller niche stores too along both sides of the street.

The **Main Street Chamber of Commerce** is where you can pickup items that you buy during the day instead of carrying them around the park.

In addition to the attractions listed on the next page, you can enjoy **Harmony Barber Shop** (a real barber shop - reservations are highly recommended at 407-W-DISNEY) and the **Main Street Vehicles**, which you can ride up and down Main Street, U.S.A. if you prefer to give your feet a rest.

DINING:

Tony's Town Square Restaurant - Table Service, Disney Dining Plan accepted, Italian food, entrées are $13-$30.
Main Street Bakery - Quick Service, Disney Dining Plan accepted, serves Starbucks products and bakery goods, sandwiches are $5, drinks are $2-$5.
Plaza Ice Cream Parlor - Snacks, Disney Dining Plan accepted, ice creams are $4-$5.
The Plaza Restaurant - Table Service, Disney Dining Plan accepted, entrées are $12-$18.
Casey's Corner - Quick Service, Disney Dining Plan accepted, entrées are $8-$10.
The Crystal Palace - Character Buffet, Disney Dining Plan accepted, $25 at breakfast, $28 at lunch and $38 at dinner per adult.

Main Street U.S.A. Railroad Station

No	None	No	Up to 20 minutes	15 minutes or less

What is Fastpass+?

This is a free time-saving service that allows you to reserve a time to ride an attraction instead of simply waiting in a queue line. See Chapter 12 for the full details.

Hop aboard the Walt Disney World Railroad for a circular tour around Magic Kingdom Park on a classic steam locomotive.

The Railroad is a relaxing way to get around the park with several stations. At each of these stations you can get on or off - the other stations are located in Frontierland and Fantasyland.

The full tour of the park takes approximately 20 minutes to complete, with trains every five minutes or so, but you are free to get on and off at whichever station you want. You can also stay on all the way around if you wish.

The Railroad does not operate during parades as the floats need to cross its tracks to access the main park.

Sorcerers of the Magic Kingdom

'Sorcerers of the Magic Kingdom' is an interactive card game where you venture from land to land in the Magic Kingdom Park finding portals. Once at a portal hold up your magic game cards and in-park screens will activate. Your cards will then help you defeat the Disney villains.

The more you play the game, the harder it gets, so you can progress throughout your trip.

To play, simply pick up your complimentary playing cards from the Firehouse on Main Street, U.S.A. Here you are given a map and full instructions.

This experience is included in your park admission at no extra charge and it is a great way to spend time in the parks without waiting in line. Guests can get five new random cards to add to their roster each day – the game is a collector's dream with over 70 cards to collect.

Town Square Theater

Fastpass+: Yes

Meet Mickey Mouse backstage at the Town Square Theater and create memories that last a lifetime. While you are at it, grab some photos too!

Surprisingly, the queue lines are bearable with wait times rarely being above 30 minutes.

Other characters also meet at this location periodically.

Frontierland

Step in and be transported to the old Wild West of the United States.

Big Thunder Mountain Railroad

| FP Yes | 40" | 📷 Yes | ✓ 4 minutes | ⏳ 90 to 120 minutes |

Jump aboard a family roller coaster sure to bring a smile to everyone's face.

This ride lasts about just under 4 minutes, which is unusually long for a roller coaster.

As you venture through the mine, you will see geysers, dynamite, western towns, flooding caves, bats and more!

The standby queue line (not Fastpass+) even has some interactive elements to help pass the time.

This is a great family ride which is relatively tame as roller coasters go, and a way to get kids interested in riding something more exhilarating.

Tom Sawyer Island

Tom Sawyer Island is an adventure and exploration area set in the heart of Frontierland.

The island is surrounded by the Rivers of America and to access the island you board a raft in Frontierland.

The island is suitable for people of all ages to enjoy and includes many areas to explore, including caves, a fort, bridges and even a mill.

As this is an open exploration area there are no waits to experience this area - for the raft crossing, you will have to wait a few minutes for the next boat.

Frontierland Shootin' Arcade

This is a shooting gallery like is seen at many fairgrounds; here it is themed to America's Wild West.

Unusually, there is an extra charge to use this shooting gallery - it is not included in regular park admission.

Splash Mountain

| FP Yes | 40" | 📷 Yes | ✓ 7 minutes | ⧖ 90 to 120 minutes |

Hop on a ride inspired by Br'er Rabbit's adventure and the *Song of the South* movie.

Splash Mountain is a log flume-style ride with a long indoor portion that follows the story of the movie. The ride is great fun with music, animatronics and small indoor drops to enjoy along the way – then, as the action heats up, you plummet down a 52-foot drop at the end and discover why this is called Splash Mountain.

Surprisingly, you do not usually get very wet on this ride, it is more of a spray than a soak – unlike its Disneyland counterpart in California, which leaves riders soaked through. However, there is always a chance you will come out drenched so you will want to leave your electronics and valuables with a non-rider.

Country Bear Jamboree

| FP No | None | 📷 No | ✓ 16 mins | ⧖ Until next show |

The Country Bear Jamboree is a sit-down theatre-show style attraction with pre-recorded singing from a series of animatronic bears.

To be honest, it is probably our least favorite attraction in the Magic Kingdom as it is very outdated and has never resonated with us.

On the other hand, it does provide shelter from the rain and heat, and allows for a sit-down break with no queue lines. Kids may also be amused.

Go in if you have the time, but do not make it a priority and do not expect any miracles from the show.

Dining:

Golden Oak Outpost - Snacks and Quick Service, Disney Dining Plan accepted, nuggets and sandwiches are $5-$10
Pecos Bill Tall Tale Inn and Cafe - Quick Service, Disney Dining Plan accepted, entrées are priced at $10-$15
Westward Ho Refreshments - Snacks, Disney Dining Plan accepted, $6.49 for a corn dog, $3 for chips and $3-$4 for drinks

Magic Kingdom Park

Liberty Square

Travel to colonial America in this unique land that cannot be found in any other Disney park around the world.

The Hall of Presidents

| FP No | None | 📷 No | ⏵ 22 minutes | ⏳ Until next show |

This show features audio animatronics of all 44 US presidents, as well as multimedia elements showcasing snippets of America's political history.

Children, and those who are less politically minded, are unlikely to be entertained. However, fierce patriots will likely enjoy the show.

The animatronics are incredibly advanced and are spookily life-like.

The attraction features a speech from current US president, Donald Trump.

Liberty Square Riverboat

| FP No | None | 📷 No | ⏵ 13 minutes | ⏳ Until next boat |

Sail around Tom Sawyer Island on a leisurely cruise on the Liberty Square riverboat. There is a very limited amount of seating and most space is standing room on this cruise.

Closing times vary seasonally and a sign at the loading area will list the time of the day's last trip, as well as the frequency of departures (usually every half hour).

Haunted Mansion

| FP Yes | None | 📷 No | ✓ 8 minutes | ⧖ 30 to 45 minutes |

Haunted Mansion is a beloved Disney classic that should not be missed.

Despite its name and its imposing facade, this is in not a horror-maze or a horror ride – it is a gentle ride with tongue-in-cheek humor.

There are no jump scares but the spooky atmosphere and loud laughter during the initial section may frighten younger children, as well as the pop-up ghosts during the graveyard scenes of the ride itself. You should also be aware that it is very dark inside.

Once you step foot into the mansion and explore the entrance area, you will be lead to "Doom Buggies" to sit in. These are small vehicles that tilt and rotate as you go through various scenes of the mansion.

You will see ghosts dancing, singing busts, a ghostly seance, ravens and much more.

Like all the lands in Magic Kingdom, Liberty Square is well themed. Here, the area is filled with details from the colonial era - many guests miss these. For example, the Liberty Bell in Magic Kingdom is one of 50 created in 1976; it was donated by the state of Pennsylvania as they already had the real one there.

Another detail can be seen on the ground. In colonial America, there was no indoor plumbing, and so residents at the time would throw their human waste into the streets - hence the brown streak in the center of the pathways in this area. This is also why there are no restrooms in this area of the park.

Dining:

Columbia Harbour House - Snacks and Quick Service, Disney Dining Plan accepted, does not serve breakfast, entrées are $9-$15

The Diamond Horseshoe Revue - Table Service, Disney Dining Plan accepted, does not serve breakfast. The set menu is $36 per adult and $20 per child.

Liberty Tree Tavern - Table Service, Disney Dining Plan accepted, entrées are $16-$23 for lunch, and $32-$38 for an all-you-can-eat family style meal for adults and $16-$21 for kids.

Liberty Square Tavern - Snacks, Disney Dining Plan accepted, hot dogs are $7.50, bacon skewers are $8 and drinks are $4-$5, fruits and other snacks are also available

Sleepy Hollow - Snacks, Disney Dining Plan accepted, waffles are $5-$9, funnel cakes are $7-$8, corn dogs are $8.50, and drinks are $3-$5.50

Magic Kingdom Park

Adventureland

Enter this land for an exciting time exploring worlds far, far away...

Pirates of the Caribbean

FP: Yes | Ruler: None | Camera: No | Clock: 8 mins | Hourglass: 20 to 45 mins

Ahoy me hearties! Set sail through the world of the 'Pirates of the Caribbean'.

Featuring the characters from the famous "Pirates of the Caribbean" blockbusters, as well as original characters that inspired the hit movies, this is a fun water flume ride through pirate-filled scenes with a small drop to add a thrill element too.

Guests board boats and sail by scenes with amazing animatronic characters. Well-known songs are played throughout the attraction adding to the Pirate-like atmosphere.

The original version of this ride in Disneyland was the final attraction Walt Disney supervised the creation, making this something truly special in the world of Disney theme parks.

Located right next door to *Pirates of the Caribbean*, young guests can take part in **The Pirate's League** and be transformed into a pirate complete with make-up and accessories. Various packages are on offer and reservations can be made up to 180 days in advance at 407-WDW-STYLE. Prices are $40 to $100.

The Magic Carpets of Aladdin

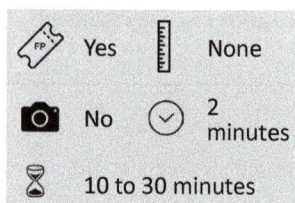

FP: Yes | Ruler: None | Camera: No | Clock: 2 minutes | Hourglass: 10 to 30 minutes

Hop aboard one of Aladdin's magic carpets and fly across Adventureland. This is a gentle ride and is very similar to Dumbo in Fantasyland.

Swiss Family Robinson Treehouse

This elaborately themed walkthrough attraction allows you to enter the Robinson's treehouse and venture from room to room seeing how they built their home following a shipwreck, making the most of nature around them.

There is no wait to explore this area and it is a good way to spend a few minutes.

Enchanted Tiki Room

A Walt Disney original attraction, step into the frankly bewildering world of singing flowers and birds in the Enchanted Tiki Room. It is perhaps Walt Disney World's most bewildering attraction, and in our opinion is in need of a replacement for today's generation.

A Pirate's Adventure: Treasures of the Seven Seas

This interactive game will have you exploring Adventureland looking for hidden treasures as you take on one of the five tasks dotted around the land.

When you begin, you will receive a magic talisman, as well as a map to help you along your way finding treasure.

Once you have found a spot, touch your talisman and see how you change Adventureland around you.

Each mission lasts 15 to 20 minutes and it is a fun way to add a unique experience to your day without needing to wait in a queue line.

Top Tip: Complete 3 out of 5 missions and you will get a bonus FastPass+ for *Pirates of The Caribbean*.

Jungle Cruise

Yes | None | No | 10 minutes | 45 to 90 minutes

Jump aboard and set sail through jungles across the world, with a skipper who just cannot help but tell the corniest jokes you have ever heard. Along the way you will see a variety of animatronic animals.

As each boat has its own individual skipper the ride experience can really vary from an outrageously hilarious trip to one where the guide offers minimal enthusiasm.

The queue line is fairly tedious with nothing much to see or do, so we recommend you make a Fastpass+ reservation for this attraction.

DINING:
Aloha Isle - Snacks, DDP accepted, dole whips and floats are $5-$7, drinks are $3-$4
Jungle Navigation Co., Ltd. Skipper Canteen - Table Service, DDP accepted, African, American, Asian and Latin cuisine, entrées are $18-$35
Sunshine Tree Terrace - Snacks, DDP accepted, desserts are $4-$6, drinks are $3-$5
Tortuga Tavern - Snacks and Quick Service, DDP accepted, Mexican cuisine, entrées are $9-$12.

Fantasyland

Welcome to the place where you can let your imagination run wild in Disney classics. This is also the place for the smaller members of the family.

Cinderella Castle

Step inside Cinderella's castle and walk under the entranceway across the moat and into Fantasyland.

Standing at 189 feet tall, Cinderella Castle is the central icon of the Magic Kingdom and indeed the whole of Walt Disney World.

As you cross the drawbridge and walk through the castle, be sure to look at the incredibly detailed mosaics around you.

Unlike some of the other Disney castles such as those at the Disneyland Resort and Disneyland Paris, you cannot visit the area inside the castle upstairs. The only exception is if you are dining at the Cinderella's Royal Table restaurant which includes appearances from the Disney princesses and select other characters.

Inside the castle on the first floor, you will find the **Bibbidi Bobbidi Boutique**, a makeover salon, where little girls can be transformed into princesses complete with make-up, a Disney costume dress and a hair do.

Packages for Bibbidi Bobbidi Boutique vary between $65 and $450, plus tax, depending on what your princess chooses to do.

Boys can take part in the form of the rather reasonably priced "Knight Package" for $20 plus tax. It includes hairstyling with gel, confetti, as well as a sword and shield to keep. A deluxe package is sold at $80.

Reservations can be made up to 180 days in advance and are strongly recommended by calling 407-WDW-STYLE or 407-939-7895.

Prince Charming Regal Carrousel

 No   None   No   90 secs   Less than 10 mins

Ride a beautiful horse in the heart of the Magic Kingdom.

This is a beautiful vintage carousel, which pre-dates the Magic Kingdom and is now over 100 years old.

The carousel is fun to ride for every member of the family and wait times never seem to be more than 5 or 10 minutes.

For a different experience, visit the carousel at night and get to see it all lit up!

Note: This ride does not operate immediately before, during or after any firework shows.

Mad Tea Party

A standard fairground ride where you ride in a teacup and spin.

If you want to go faster, just turn the wheel in the center of the cup – you can reach some dizzying speeds.

The wait times are never too long for this attraction and if the posted wait is anything more than 15 minutes, we recommend you simply come back later in the day.

Yes | None | No | 90 secs | Less than 5 mins

Princess FairyTale Hall

Meet and greet Disney princesses in this most royal of settings.

Choose one of the two queue lines: one is to meet Cinderella and a visiting princess; the other is to meet Rapunzel and a visiting princess.

The interior of the meet and greet is lavish with stonewalls, chandeliers and Cinderella themed stained-glass windows in the queue line. You will even get a chance to see Cinderella's glass slipper!

Yes | None | Yes | 2 mins | 30 to 90 mins

Please note that the ever-popular Anna and Elsa do not meet here, but at the Norway pavilion at Epcot.

Casey Jr. Splash 'N' Soak Station

Located in the Storybook Circus area, this play area is a great place to cool down.

There are streams of water from the giraffes and other animals and even a smoky mist from Casey Jr.'s chimney.

As this is an open area, there is no wait to get in, making this the perfect place to let the young ones play.

"it's a small world"

One of the most memorable attractions, "it's a small world" features hundreds of singing dolls singing a catchy tune about the uniting of the world.

Your cruise travels leisurely around scenes from across the world and this is a fun ride, especially for younger kids. The queue line for this ride moves very quickly. This is a great Disney classic, which, although not based on any film franchise, is one of the many "must-dos" for most visitors.

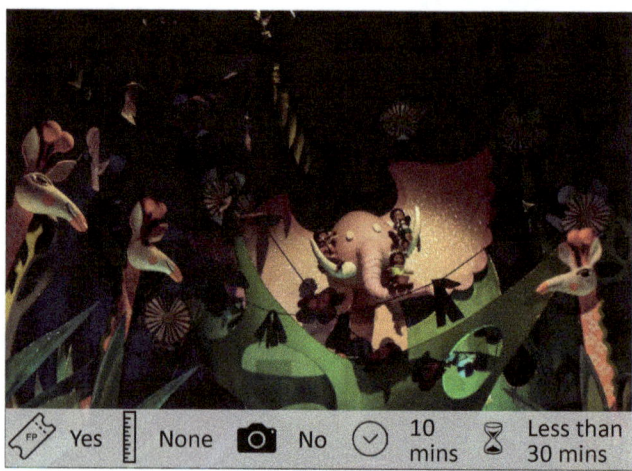

Yes | None | No | 10 mins | Less than 30 mins

Seven Dwarfs Mine Train

This fun roller coaster contains both inside dark ride elements and outside roller coaster sections taking you into the world of Snow White and even the Seven Dwarf's mine where "a million diamonds shine".

The ride cars are unique in that they swing as guests go around bends like real mine carts would.

The thrill level is just below Big Thunder Mountain but a step up from The Barnstormer. It also fits perfectly in the middle for the height limit – a true family ride.

The queue line features interactive elements

Yes | 38" | Yes | 3 mins | 90 to 120 mins

including an area where you can wash and sort jewels, spin barrels, and interact with musical water features.

Under the Sea - Journey of the Little Mermaid

Step into Ariel's undersea home as you board a clamshell and become part of her world.

Under the Sea is our favorite dark ride in all of the Walt Disney World Resort as it is perfectly executed and the ride feels like a 'modern classic'.

The storytelling is great, the animatronics are amazing, the music is exceptional and the ride entertains throughout while moving slowly and steadily enough to not frighten young ones.

Do watch out for the incredible appearance of Ursula if you have any sensitive guests in your group, although the moment is quickly over.

Even the queue line is fun with incredible theming, star character appearances from Scuttle and an interactive game to play where you have to spot the crabs.

| FP Yes | None | No | 5 mins | 20 to 45 mins |

Top Tip: In the last hour of park operation, this attraction is a 'walk-on', meaning that you will not need to wait to board. If the wait is over 25 minutes during the day, we recommend you wait until the evening to ride.

Mickey's Philharmagic

Philharmagic is, in our opinion, by far the Walt Disney World Resort's best 4D show, and one that should not be missed.

The story is that you are attending Goofy's opera performance with Mickey's Philharmonic orchestra. When Donald gets involved, however, things get a little out of hand and you end up on an adventure travelling through a world of Disney classic movies.

With an air-conditioned queue line and theatre, shelter from the rain and a fantastic musical movie, it is easy to see why this attraction has one of the highest guest satisfaction ratings in the whole of the Magic Kingdom.

Do not miss this show – it usually has very short waits!

| FP Yes | None | No | 10 mins | Less than 15 mins |

Top Tip: At the end of the show, when Donald flies off the screen and the curtain goes down, take a look at the back of the theatre for an extra special surprise.

Magic Kingdom Park

Enchanted Tales with Belle

An interactive adventure where you are taken into Maurice's cottage, and are magically transported (in a mind-blowing fashion) to the Beast's castle.

Once there, you will meet Madame Wardrobe and even have a chance to surprise Belle. This is a meet and greet unlike any other!

Not everyone in the group must take part surprising Belle, but you *can* volunteer to help with the surprise if you want. If you do not wish to take part, you can simply sit back and enjoy the show.

Even if you do not fancy meeting the princesses, we highly recommend paying

| Yes | None | Yes | 15 mins | 30 to 60 mins |

this attraction a visit – it is definitely worth the wait, with about 15 minutes of guest experience when you get inside and the attraction includes some incredible special effects.

Top Tip: Make sure you get a good view of the mirror behind the Cast Member when they are doing their speech – you will be astounded at what it can do!

The Lumière animatronic in the main show room is not to be missed either!

The Many Adventures of Winnie the Pooh

| Yes | None | No | 3 minutes | 45 to 75 minutes |

Hop inside one of Pooh's "hunny pots" and explore one of his many adventures.

This is a gentle ride where you venture through Pooh's stories; it includes slight rocking and jumping motions to enhance the experience.

As well as the popular characters, the ride is filled with bright colors that should excite the little ones.

One of the best things is the interactive queue line where there are games to play to help pass the time, from a bee roller coaster to smearing the honey off a wall – it is fun and helps the wait times feel shorter.

The Barnstormer

A small roller coaster for kids with one drop and a few turns.

The ride is good fun but it is very short, and rougher than it appears from the outside.

It is a good starter coaster for kids, and it has a very low minimum height limit meaning that almost anyone of a suitable age can enjoy it.

| Yes | 35" | No | 1 min | 25 to 45 mins |

Peter Pan's Flight

Peter Pan's Flight is one of the Magic Kingdom's most popular rides. You board a flying pirate ship and take a voyage through the world of Peter Pan and Never Never Land.

The scenes are both besides you and below you, and the interior to this ride is stunning, from the moment you step in.

This ride is incredibly popular, so a Fastpass+ reservation is a must.

The low capacity of the ride, coupled with the immense

Yes | None | No | 5 mins | 90 to 120 mins

popularity of the characters, causes long waits to form. However, guests in the standby line are able to enjoy a fantastic interactive queue line that takes you through the Darlings' nursery.

Note: If you are afraid of heights, this ride may not be suitable for you as the ships give the sensation of flight. At times you are several feet off the ground.

Dumbo: The Flying Elephant

Dumbo is one of the most popular rides at Magic Kingdom Park.

As you gently spin, use the lever at front of the seats in each Dumbo elephant to lift your Dumbo up or down! When you are in-flight the ride offers nice views of the surrounding area, as well as a whole lot of fun.

Due to its popularity amongst both children and adults alike, there are now two sets of Dumbos and wait times are much shorter.

Yes | None | No | 90 secs | 20 to 45 mins

Disney has created a clever waiting system in the main tent whereby you are given a pager. While waiting, kids can play in a play area - once it is your turn to board you will be paged. You forget you are queuing!

DINING:
Be Our Guest Restaurant - Quick Service [breakfast and lunch] and Table Service [2 credits - dinner], DDP accepted – the breakfast prix fixe meal is $25 for adults and $14 for children, lunch entrées are $13-$17, dinner prix fixe meals are $60 per adult and $36 per child. Reservations are required for all meals, including quick service..
Cinderella's Royal Table - Table Service, DDP accepted, breakfast prices are $45-$65 per adult ($35 to $45 per child), lunch and dinner is $65-$80 per adult and $45-$65 per child.
Gaston's Tavern - Snacks, DDP accepted, snacks are $4-$10, and drinks are $2.50-$13
Pinocchio Village Haus - Snacks and Quick Service, DDP accepted, entrées are $7-$13.
Prince Eric's Village Market - Snacks, DDP not accepted, snacks are $2-$7

Magic Kingdom Park

Tomorrowland

Have a taste of the future in this land that leaves today behind.

Buzz Lightyear Space Ranger Spin

Buzz Lightyear invites you to step aboard his ship and use the on-board guns to help defeat the evil emperor Zurg. By shooting the targets around you, you will be helping out Buzz and racking up points.

Different targets are worth different amounts of points and there are even hidden targets to get thousands of bonus points at once.

| Yes | None | Yes | 5 mins | 45 to 75 mins |

You can also change the direction of your Space Cruiser with the joystick in the middle of the vehicle and turn the car the other way if you spot a target your friend has not. At the end of the ride, the one with the most points wins.

It is competitive and endlessly 're-rideable'. Great fun!

Tomorrowland Transit Authority Peoplemover

| No | None | No | 10 minutes | Less than 10 minutes |

One of our favorite hidden gems at the Magic Kingdom is the Peoplemover - a relaxing way to tour Tomorrowland including seeing the inside of Space Mountain and Buzz Lightyear Space Ranger Spin!

The ten-minute ride is a chance to put up your feet. Wait times for the Peoplemover are often non-existent.

Monsters, Inc. Laugh Floor

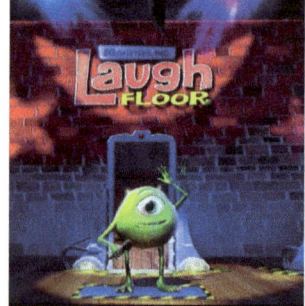

| Yes | None | No | 12 mins | 15 to 30 mins |

Step in for an interactive show with Mike Wazowski and his comical friends from 'Monsters Inc.' who are ready to interact with the audience, including you.

Get ready to laugh, play, and potentially be made fun of.

You will want to be sure you are having fun or you might have the pleasure of being dubbed by the monsters as "That Guy" during the show.

Tomorrowland Speedway

Little kids are notorious for loving little cars and this is their first chance to have a go driving for themselves.

Here, you get to cruise along at up to 7mph and enjoy the sights. Great fun for kids who are car-obsessed!

The minimum height is 54" to drive alone, and kids must be at least 32" tall to ride with an adult.

| FP Yes | See text | No | 15 mins | 15 to 30 mins |

Astro Orbiter

Above the Peoplemover is Astro Orbiter, a spinning type ride similar to *Dumbo The Flying Elephant* and *The Magic Carpets of Aladdin*.

The difference here, is that these rockets spin much faster, and you are much higher up – so high up, that you can see outside the park!

This is a fun ride but you should know that the space rockets are very small and getting two adults into one is tough! Even an adult and a child is a tight fit.

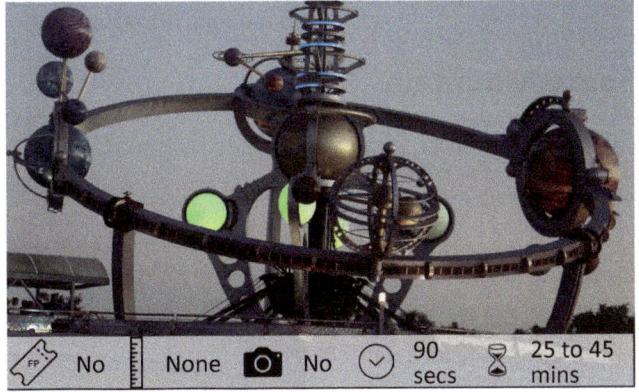

| FP No | None | No | 90 secs | 25 to 45 mins |

Walt Disney's Carousel of Progress

A classic attraction designed by Walt Disney himself, the Carousel of Progress is a touching, funny and heartwarming show that moves from scene to scene every few minutes.

You start off seeing a family at the turn of the century and see how life was like in the early 1900s, then every few minutes the carousel will rotate and you will move forward in time with the family by a few decades.

There are some great in-jokes and it is fun to see how

FP	Height	Camera	Duration	Wait
No	None	No	20 mins	Less than 10 mins

the year 2000 ('the future') at the end was envisioned back in the 1960s.

As the song throughout the ride lets you know "There is a great big beautiful tomorrow just a dream away!"

Space Mountain

Space Mountain is a roller coaster through space designed with the family in mind - it has no loops or inversions and provides the feeling of soaring through the galactic world.

This is not the wildest thrill ride in the world, but a fun adventure nonetheless - it is still the most intense coaster at the Magic Kingdom, in our opinion.

We strongly recommend making a Fastpass+ reservation as the standby queue line is slow moving

FP	Height	Camera	Duration	Wait
Yes	40"	Yes	3 mins	90 to 120 mins

and not on that you want to be stuck in.

Alternatively, get to this ride first thing in the morning or at the end of the day to minimize your wait.

DINING:

Auntie Gravity's Galactic Goodies - Snacks, DDP accepted, desserts are $3-4, drinks are $3-$6
Cool Ship - Snacks, No DDP, drinks are $3-$5, a hot dog with chips is $9
Cosmic Ray's Starlight Café - Quick Service, DDP accepted, entrées are $10-$18
The Lunching Pad - Snacks and Quick Service, DDP accepted, entrées are $9.50-$12
Tomorrowland Terrace Restaurant - Snacks and Quick Service, DDP accepted, entrées are $10.50-$12.50

Live Entertainment

Magic Kingdom Park has plenty of entertainment offerings throughout the day - these are all included in your park admission price and you could fill almost an entire day with these alone. We recommend you show up 5 to 10 minutes in advance of the published show times to get a good view. A show times leaflet provides you with live entertainment timings for the whole week – you can get this at the entrance of the park and most in-park shops.

Flag Retreat (Main Street, U.S.A.) – Hear patriotic songs as the American flag is lowered and folded in the afternoon each day. A guest is selected to help with ceremony – this is usually an active service person or a veteran. The ceremony lasts about 15 minutes in total.

Citizens of Main Street – Meet the citizens of Main Street, U.S.A. throughout the day including the Mayor, the chief fireman and other locals.

Main Street Philharmonic at Main Street, U.S.A. – This classic band plays tunes from Disney movies.

Main Street Trolley Show – See citizens take to the streets in a 5-minute show around a horse-drawn streetcar. This show usually takes place several times in the morning.

Casey's Corner Pianist (Main Street, U.S.A.) – Several times a day, usually in the afternoon, join the pianist at Casey's Corner and listen to his tunes. He even takes song requests.

"The Muppets Present… Great Moments in American History" (New Orleans Square) – The Muppets characters tell historical tales in a hysterical fashion.

The Royal Majesty Makers (Fantasyland) – Gain a royal education through games, dancing and more with this fun crew.

Main Street Philharmonic at Storybook Circus (Fantasyland) – This classic band plays tunes from both classic and new Disney movies.

"A Totally Tomorrowland Christmas Show" (Tomorrowland – Holiday season only) – Join this intergalactic Christmas party where Stitch jets off to find Santa. This show is 20 minutes in length.

> **STAGE SHOWS:**
>
> **Mickey's Royal Friendship Faire** – This 20-minute show plays right in front of Cinderella Castle and features Mickey Mouse and his friends, along with characters from some of Disney's newest classics: "The Princess and the Frog," "Tangled" and "Frozen."
>
> **Cinderella's/A Frozen Holiday Wish** (Holiday Season only) – See the Fairy Godmother grant Cinderella's wish as she magically turns Cinderella Castle into a glittering, icy palace! This show is 10 minutes in length. In the past, this show has included Anna and Elsa from Disney's Frozen as the main characters instead of Cinderella and the Fairy Godmother.
>
> **"Celebrate the Season" Show** (Holiday season only) – This 25-minute show in front of Cinderella Castle features Mickey and Minnie as they spread some holiday cheer, including classic Disney songs.

Magic Kingdom Park

Parades

There are two parades that happen most days at the Magic Kingdom:

Disney's Festival of Fantasy Parade is a must-watch experience, and it is the park's main daily parade. It usually takes place at 2:00pm or 3:00pm daily and starts in Frontierland by Splash Mountain. It makes its way through Liberty Square, round the castle hub, and down Main Street, U.S.A.

The parade brings the magical stories of Fantasyland to life through parade floats, vibrant costumes and an original soundtrack that features beloved songs from favorite Disney films.

Ariel and friends grace a larger-than-life music box showcasing a musical party "Under the Sea", while Scottish dancers and a bagpipe-shaped float announce the arrival of Merida.

Other floats celebrate Disney Princesses and Dumbo; Peter Pan and Wendy soar above a pirate galleon; a steam punk Maleficent float is present; and Rapunzel and Flynn Rider appear too!

A Dining Package with reserved parade viewing is available at Tony's Town Square Restaurant. At the cost of $54 for adults and $19 for children (ages 3-9), the package provides an enjoyable way to combine a meal and some entertainment. Included in the package are an appetizer, entrée, dessert, non-alcoholic beverage and vouchers for watching the parade from its reserved viewing location.

The **Move It! Shake It! Dance and Play It! Party** happens up to three times a day with the main show taking place on the hub in front of Cinderella Castle. In this interactive parade the floats stop and you get to join in with the dancing.

Starting in January 2019, this will be replaced with **Move It! Shake It! MousekeDance It! Street Party** for a limited time.

During the Halloween season, you will also be able to see **Mickey's "Boo to You" Halloween Parade**, and during the Holiday season there is a special parade too, **Mickey's Once Upon a Christmastime Parade**.

Fireworks

Every evening, experience a grand finale to your Disney day with the newest—and most spectacular—fireworks showcase in Magic Kingdom history with **"Happily Ever After"**.

Happily Ever After starts with a dream... and takes you on an unforgettable journey that captures the heart, humor and heroism of many favorite Disney animated films.

This 18-minute show features more lasers, lights and projections than any other fireworks spectacular in the history of Magic Kingdom park!

Throughout Happily Ever After, you'll witness the many transformations of Cinderella Castle as it becomes a part of popular Disney stories.

Be sure to get a spot in the area in front of the castle at least 45 minutes in advance.

For the best view, you will want to be near the Casey's Corner area of Main Street, U.S.A - or anywhere in the hub area in front of the castle. Get too close though, and you miss out on the fireworks behind the castle and cannot truly appreciate the scale of the projections.

The show can also be viewed from anywhere along Main Street the Railroad Station at the entrance to the park, as well as from many hotels if high up enough and facing the correct direction. You can also view the show from almost anywhere in the park but for an optimum view, you want to be facing the castle for the projections which are a *big* part of the show.

There are seasonal changes to the fireworks too. The **'Happy HalloWishes Fireworks'** play during Disney's Halloween Season parties, and during the Christmas and Holiday season's parties, you can enjoy **'Holiday Wishes'**. On the 3rd and 4th of July you can also watch **"Disney's Celebrate America! – A Fourth of July Concert in the Sky"** fireworks.

Fireworks Dessert Party: Venture to Tomorrowland Terrace Restaurant, where a tempting array of freshly prepared desserts, seasonal fruits and flavorful cheeses awaits. As showtime nears, Cast Members will escort you to a prime standing area in the Plaza Garden for priority viewing of the nighttime fireworks spectacular. Then, watch in amazement as the skies ignite and Cinderella Castle glows with enchanting illuminations.

The Fireworks Dessert Party is priced at $69 for adults and $41 for children, tax included.

Ferrytale Fireworks – A Sparkling Dessert Cruise: Take in a breathtaking view of Magic Kingdom Park's spectacular fireworks from an exclusive spot on Seven Seas Lagoon with desserts and drinks.

Sail on an iconic, double-stack ferryboat. Decks are laden with delectable desserts inspired by the landmarks around you, as well as a fabulous fruit and cheese spread. Toast the evening with specialty beverages in souvenir glow glasses.

Enjoy this sweet ending to your day, before watching the fireworks. The medley of famous Disney songs and the voices of Disney characters are piped through the boat's sound system for this magical viewing.

This experience is offered on select dates. The cost is $99 for adults and $69 ages 3 to 9, including tax and gratuity.

Chapter Eight | Epcot

Epcot

Epcot was the second theme park to open at the Walt Disney World Resort, opening in 1982. Its name is an acronym and stands for the 'Experimental Prototype Community of Tomorrow', Walt Disney's vision for the future of cities.

Although, Epcot never become a city of tomorrow, today's version of Epcot is still one of the most unique concepts for a theme park in existence anywhere in the world.

The park is split into two halves:
- *Future World* is where world class attractions take you into the future and beyond. Here you can soar around the world on a paraglider, enter a futuristic test track and blast off into space.
- *World Showcase* is made up of Pavilions representing different countries. Here you immersed into different cultures with food, attractions, architecture and more. Each person working at the pavilions has actually been recruited to work there for a year by Disney from their own country for an extra layer of authenticity.

Future World

Spaceship Earth

Inside the giant geodesic sphere (or the golf ball as most guests call it), there is a ride taking you on a slow moving journey from the dawn of time to the internet age. It is a fun and fascinating tale that is worth experiencing.

Towards the end, there is even a fun interaction portion where you can choose your future on a touchscreen.

We recommend riding this attraction later in the day as many guests line up for it at park opening as it is located right at the entrance - due to its nature, the ride never stops loading and unloading so lines constantly move.

In the afternoon and evenings there is very unlikely to be any wait at all to get on the ride.

FP: Yes | None | Camera: Yes | 13 mins | Less than 30 mins

Epcot Character Spot

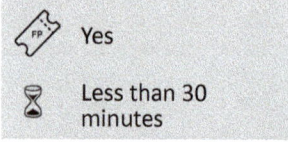

Yes
Less than 30 minutes

This is the place to meet Mickey, Minnie and other classic Disney characters in one spot.

Baymax from Big Hero 6 can also be met here, as can Joy and Sadness from Inside Out.

This air-conditioned character location does not usually have long lines and it is a great chance to meet lots of characters in just one go. If lines are long, come back later.

Magic Eye Theater

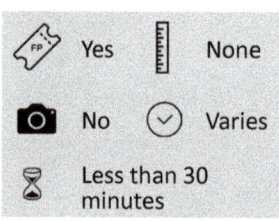

FP: Yes | None
Camera: No | Varies
Less than 30 minutes

The Magic Eye Theater shows a rotating set of short films as part of the "Disney & Pixar Short Film Festival".

Occasionally, extended movie previews are also shown at this location.

This is far from a must do attraction, in our opinion.

Club Cool

Technically this is a store, but a large attraction of this location is the fact that you can sample Coca-Cola Company products from across the globe for free.

Once inside, grab a taster cup, fill it up from one of the main fountains and drink - it's free and unlimited!

Some of the flavors are much nicer than others – we love the Watermelon drink! Part of the fun is figuring out your favorites.

Test Track

A fun family thrill ride that takes you into the world of Chevrolet. In the queue line you design your own vehicle on a touchscreen, which is then virtually tested against other riders' vehicles throughout the ride.

The ride itself is a fun exploration of how different factors can influence a car and its capability, efficiency, responsiveness, and power.

This attraction is great fun but beware that the ride is intense. It is the fastest ride in all of the Walt Disney World Resort and reaches speeds exceeding 100km/h.

In the Single Rider line, waits rarely exceed 30 minutes.

| | Yes | 40" | Yes | 60 to 120 mins |

The Seas with Nemo and Friends

A slow moving clam shell ride past one of the biggest aquariums in the world. Stare in to take a look at the fish, and look out for characters from Pixar's *Finding Nemo* woven into the ride storyline mixed in the same tanks as real fish.

After riding, enjoy *Seabase* - a 5.7-million-liter aquarium with interactive exhibitions, tutorials and glass panes to see straight into the water and observe its inhabitants.

| | Yes | None | No | 4 mins | Less than 20 mins |

Turtle Talk with Crush

| | Yes | None | No | 12 mins | Less than 20 mins |

A "totally cool" show with Finding Nemo's turtle Crush! This interactive show gets adults and kids alike to speak to Crush and ask him questions about the turtle world; meanwhile Crush has some questions for you about the human world.

It is a whole lot of fun if you are willing to get involved. You might even learn to speak whale!

As well as characters from "Finding Nemo", others from "Finding Dory" make appearances.

Mission: SPACE

Soar into space as you are put into an astronaut's shoes at Epcot. Get ready to experience the same level of G-force a professional feels and to pilot a space shuttle on your mission to Mars.

Due to its intensity, Disney offers two versions of the attraction. The "less intense" green version is still reasonably intense as simulators go.

The "more intense" orange version is the same as the green version, but the ride vehicles also spins rapidly to create a centrifugal force that pushes and pulls you from your seat making for a more intense experience. This more accurately reflects the feeling of zero gravity but is more likely to induce

Yes | 44" | No | 6 mins | 20 to 60 mins

nausea.

We strongly recommend you do not eat before riding this attraction, or at the very least allow a few hours to digest your food, as this ride is known for inducing motion sickness - even in people who do not usually suffer from the condition.

Be sure to read all the health warnings before boarding.

The post-ride area is called the *Advanced Training Lab*. This is an interactive indoor play area for all ages where you can put your space skills to the test. There is lots of fun to be had here and it is a good shelter from the rain.

Journey into Imagination with Figment

Yes | 44" | No | 8 minutes | Less than 10 minutes

This is perhaps the strangest attraction in all of Walt Disney World.

Your friend Figment (a purple dragon) wants to test out all five of your senses in this unusual slow moving ride. It is a bizarre experience that is worth doing at least once.

The post-ride area is called *ImageWorks*, and is a variety of fun interactive games – mostly to do with music.

The post-ride area can also be entered via the shop if you do not wish to ride the attraction.

Soarin' Around the World

One of Epcot's most popular attractions, Soarin' gives you the chance to experience what it is like to fly and hang glide over places around the world.

It is a truly immersive experience with smells and slow movement to match a giant on-screen video, creating an incredibly realistic sensation of flight. If you are scared of heights this ride is most definitely not for you.

For us, this is truly one of the best attractions in the whole park - the concept is simple but the execution is excellent.

Yes | 40" | No | 5 mins | 60 to 90 mins

Living with the Land

A slow cruise with narration through greenhouses, fish farms and more.

Learn about the land, how humans use it and all it provides. Witness plant-growing technology techniques such as hydroponics - where plants are grown in water without soil.

A "Behind the Seeds" paid walking tour is also available from the counter by *Soarin' Around the World*.

Yes | None | No | 14 mins | Less than 30 mins

DINING:
Coral Reef Restaurant - Living Seas pavilion, Table Service, DDP accepted, entrées are $24-$35.
Electric Umbrella - Innoventions East, Snacks and Quick Service, DDP accepted, entrées are $8.50 to $14
Fountain View - Snacks, DDP accepted, desserts and Starbucks beverages $3-$6
Garden Grill - Table Service, DDP accepted, breakfast, lunch and dinner served family style with characters, breakfast is $19 for kids and $32 for adults, lunch and dinner is $19-$27 for kids and $38-$45 for adults.
Sunshine Seasons Food Court - Snacks and Quick Service, DDP accepted, entrées are priced at $8-$14.
Taste Track - Snacks and Quick Service, DDP accepted, prices vary seasonally.

World Showcase

Leaving Future World behind, The World Showcase is the second half of Epcot. Split into eleven countries located around a central lagoon, the World Showcase is your opportunity to explore different corners of the world, all just a stroll away from each other.

Explore World Showcase's pavilions and move from Canada to the UK in just a couple of minutes or travel to China and discover new cultures.

Shop, dine, experience attractions and speak to real representatives from the countries.

Note: With the exception of some smaller food stands and dining locations, World Showcase and its attractions open at 11:00am, and not at 9:00am with Future World.

The exceptions are the Norway and Mexico pavilions that open at 9:00am, including their attractions.

If you are staying at the hotels in the Epcot area, you may use the park's International Gateway entrance from park opening, and walk from World Showcase to Future World.

World Showcase Activities

Disney Phineas and Ferb: Agent P's World Showcase Adventure

With recruiting locations across the World Showcase, you can join Phineas and Ferb by becoming a special agent and exploring several countries' pavilions while completing missions on a specially designed phone.

This is a great attraction for entertaining the kids who might otherwise find the World Showcase area a little boring.

Kidcot Fun Stops:

Designed for the youngest members of your party, each country around the World Showcase features these "fun stops".

Each stop has a variety of activities for children to take part in as they make their way around the World Showcase.

Mexico

Guests who enter World Showcase from Future World and start their journey by going left (clockwise) around the lagoon, will reach this pavilion first. Inside the pyramid-shaped building there is a large indoor, covered area with restaurants, shops and the 'Gran Fiesta Tour' attraction. This pavilion opens at 9:00am.

Gran Fiesta Tour Starring The Three Caballeros

A slow moving boat ride through classic Mexican landscapes.

While you are admiring the scenery, José Carioca and Panchit (two of the Three Cabelleros) are on the lookout for Donald Duck - can you find him by the end of the ride?

This is a gentle and calm adventure that rarely has a wait time.

We recommend this gentle cruise if you fancy a relaxing ride that is family friendly

- plus there is some fun lively music. It is a bit like "it's small world" but just for Mexico.

FP: No | Ruler: None | Camera: No | Duration: 8 mins | Wait: Less than 10 mins

Mexico Folk Art Gallery

This gallery features temporary exhibitions about Mexico and its culture.

> **DINING:**
> **San Angel Inn Restaurante** - Table Service, DDP accepted, entrées are $13-$36
> **La Cava de Tequila** - Bar, No DDP, drinks are $13.50-18
> **La Cantina de San Angel** - Quick Service, DDP accepted, entrées are $8-$13.50
> **La Hacienda de San Angel** - Table Service, DDP accepted, dinner only, entrées are $18-$34

Norway

The Norway pavilion is arguably the most popular around the World Showcase due to the introduction of a Frozen attraction and a meet-and-greet with the famous sisters from the Frozen movie. This pavilion opens at 9:00am.

Frozen Ever After

This attraction is an incredible adventure fit for the entire family with the most incredible animatronics and technology ever seen on a Disney attraction.

Guests are transported to the 'Winter in Summer Celebration', visit Elsa's Ice Palace and the North Mountain, along with other locations, before returning to the Bay of Arendelle. A photo is taken for guests wearing a MagicBand.

This is an absolute must do

FP: Yes | Height: None | Photo: Yes | Wait: 5 mins | Duration: 60 to 90 mins

attraction. Minimize waits by getting here when the park opens, or reserve Fastpass+ well in advance.

Royal Sommerhus

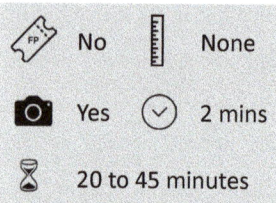

FP: No | Height: None | Photo: Yes | Wait: 2 mins | Duration: 20 to 45 minutes

A well-themed and fun meet-and-greet with the Frozen sisters, Anna and Elsa.

Stave Church Gallery

This gallery showcases Norwegian artefacts. Many of these details inspired the writers behind the hit Disney movie 'Frozen'.

Exhibitions change periodically.

DINING:

Akershus Royal Banquet Hall - Buffet with Characters, DDP accepted, breakfast is $47-$55 per adult and $28-$33 per child, lunch & dinner is $54-$65 per adult and $35-$40 for kids.
Kringla Bakeri Og Kafe - Snacks and Quick Service, DDP accepted, entrées are $8-$9.50

China

The Chinese pavilion is one of the most serene and authentic to explore. Although the main shop isn't huge, the two attractions inside the pavilion's main building and the variety of eateries more than make up for this.

Reflections of China

'Reflections of China' is a fascinating 360-degree movie retold by a Chinese poet inspiring you to visit this wonderful country.

Along the journey you can expect to see The Forbidden City, Hong Kong, Shanghai, The Great Wall of China and many more locations. This show is standing room only.

No | None | No | 12 mins | Less than 15 mins

House of the Whispering Willows

This walk-through attraction features temporary exhibitions about China. At the time of writing, the exhibition is about Disney's newest resort, Shanghai Disneyland.

DINING:
Joy of Tea - Snacks, No DDP, serves drinks, desserts and snacks, snacks are $4-$11
Lotus Blossom Café - Quick Service, DDP accepted, entrées are $10-$11
Nine Dragons Restaurant - Table Service, DDP accepted, entrées are $16-$24 at lunch and $16-$34 at dinner

Germany

This pavilion only has a small outdoor area, but contains the huge Biergarten restaurant. There are stores here, but there are no attractions.

DINING:

Biergarten Restaurant - Buffet, DDP accepted, adult meals are $28-$36 and children's are $17-$21 at lunch, the dinner buffet is $41 for adults and $22 for children
Sommerfest - Snacks and Quick Service, DDP accepted, entrées $4.50-$10.50

Italy

Enjoy the photo opportunities, dine and shop. There are no attractions here.

DINING:

Gelati - Snacks, No DDP, ice creams are $5-$10
Tutto Gusto Wine Cellar - Bar, No DDP, small dishes are $12-$26
Tutto Italia - Table Service, DDP accepted, entrées are $19-$35 at lunch and $25-$35 at dinner
Via Napoli Pizzeria - Table Service, DDP accepted, individual pizzas start at $19, and large family-size pizzas go for up to $48.

The American Adventure

The host pavilion houses an opulent building on two levels that is much larger than it appears from the outside – it houses the two attractions listed here. The American Gardens Theater, by the waterside, hosts live performances.

The American Adventure

Before watching this multimedia show, explore the inside of the pavilion building to find paintings and quotes from influential American figures throughout history.

Be sure to get to the building well before showtime for the incredible "Voices of Liberty" a cappella choir who sings patriotic songs, as well as Disney classics before most performances.

No | None | No | 28 mins | At set times

The show itself is a retelling of the U.S.A.'s history. It is educational and well-paced, but won't thrill anyone.

American Heritage Gallery

This gallery features temporary exhibits covering American history.

> **DINING:**
> **Funnel Cake Kiosk** - Snacks, No DDP, funnel cakes are $7-$11.50
> **Liberty Inn** - Snacks and Quick Service, DDP accepted for drinks and desserts only, entrées are $8.50-$14

Japan

The Japan pavilion is one of our favorites. It is serene, filled with beautiful photo opportunities, and you really do feel transported away from a busy theme park. Part of the reason for this is that there is no major attraction here. Instead the majority of the pavilion is a huge shop that sells everything Japanese, from food to lampshades, and pearls to comic books.

Bijutsu-kan Gallery

This gallery features exhibits covering Japanese history, which change regularly.

> **DINING:**
> **Kabuki Café** - Snacks, No DDP, snacks are $5-$5.50
> **Katsura Grill** - Quick Service, DDP accepted, entrées are $9-$14
> **Teppan Edo** - Table Service, DDP accepted, entrées are $24-$37 at lunch and dinner
> **Tokyo Dining** - Table Service, DDP accepted, entrées are $14-$34

Morocco

The Morocco pavilion is absolutely stunning and immediately stands out as one of the most authentic-looking pavilions. From the small passageways to the marketplace area with street sellers, it all feels very real.

Gallery of Arts and History

This gallery features temporary exhibits covering Moroccan history.

DINING:
Tangierine Café - Quick Service, DDP accepted, entrées are $9-$18
Restaurant Marrakesh - Table Service, DDP accepted, entrées are $19-$25 at lunch and $22-$30 at dinner
Spice Road Table - Table Service, DDP accepted, entrées are $23-$33

France

This is another beautiful pavilion, and houses one of the World Showcase's theater shows, 'Impressions de France'. There is a perfume shop, a bakery, and more locations that make this place feel as French as possible.

Impressions de France

Explore France through a cinematic video on five screens spanning 220 degrees with well-known landmarks, and hidden gems.

Along your journey you will see the Eiffel Tower and Arc de Triomphe, the French Alps, as well as Normandy, Cannes and more.

| FP No | None | Photo No | 18 mins | Until next show |

DINING:
Chefs de France - Table Service, DDP accepted, entrées are $19-$36
Monsieur Paul - Signature Table Service Restaurant (2 credits required), DDP accepted, dinner only, entrées are $40-$44. There is also a 3-course set menu at $89.
L'Artisan des Glaces - Snacks, No DDP, ice creams are $5-$12
Les Halles Boulangerie & Patisserie - Snacks and Quick Service, entrées are $5-$10.

United Kingdom

Themed to a quaint English town, there is always a lot going on here, from the pub's atmosphere to the meet-and-greets to stage performances. There are, of course, many shops to explore. There are no attractions at the UK pavilion.

DINING:
Rose & Crown Pub & Dining Room - Table Service, DDP accepted, entrées are $20-$27
Yorkshire County Fish Shop - Quick Service, DDP accepted, meals are $11.50
UK Beer Cart - Drinks location, No DDP, alcoholic beverages are $8.50-$10.50

Canada

As we finish our clockwise tour of the World Showcase, the final pavilion is Canada. There is good theming, world class dining and an attraction.

O Canada!

No | None | No | 14 minutes | Until next show

Martin Short takes you on an amusing, albeit stereotypical, tour around Canada. This show is standing room only as it is presented in 360-degree circle-vision.

DINING:
Le Cellier Steakhouse - Table Service, DDP accepted – 2 Table Service credits required, entrées are $30-$54

More about Epcot

Transportation – World Showcase Boats

The full walk around the World Showcase Lagoon (without exploring any of the countries) loop is 1.2 miles, but if you want to get across from one side to another quickly, catch one of the boats. Boats depart from the Future World side of the lagoon and go across to the Germany and Morocco pavilions.

World Showcase Entrance

Epcot's main entrance is by Spaceship Earth leading to Future World, but the park also has a "back" entrance leading to the World Showcase located by the UK and French pavilions. It is most often used by those staying at the Boardwalk, Yacht and Beach Club, and Swan and Dolphin resorts, although anyone may use it. Boats to Disney's Hollywood Studios are by this entrance. When the Skyliner opens (see the transportation chapter), guests will arrive here.

EPCOT Live Entertainment

JAMMitors (Future World, usually by *Test Track* and *Innoventions*) – Janitors use their tools to make music.

Joyful! A Gospel Celebration of the Season (Future World Fountain stage) – This stage show is a Holiday season spectacular with live instruments and gospel-style singers.

Mariachi Cobre (Mexican pavilion) – A Mexican folk band.

Sahara Beat (Moroccan pavilion) – Dance and sing to the rhythms of Morocco.

The Jeweled Dragon Acrobats (Chinese pavilion) – This acrobatic troupe performs stunts.

Sergio (Italian pavilion) – A football juggler.

Voices of Liberty (American Adventure pavilion) – Voices of Liberty dazzle with their incredible voices, and songs from throughout U.S. history, as well as Disney songs.

Matsuriza (Japanese pavilion) – Traditional Taiko drumming.

Serveur Amusant (French pavilion) – French acrobats dazzle with incredible skills.

Rose & Crown Pub Musician (UK pavilion) – Every evening live music in played in the pub.

British Revolution (UK pavilion) – Rock out to this live band who play classic British tunes.

Bodh'aktan (Canadian Pavilion) – Seven piratical rogues who take the stage with music that combines Celtic, Trad-Quebecois, Polka, Punk, Irish Folk, Breton and Maritime.

Groovin' Alps (German pavilion) – Grab your lederhosen and get ready to dance along with this high-energy German percussion band. This group brings the sounds of the mountains to Epcot with Bavarian folk tunes played on items found on a dairy farm.

Illuminations: Reflections of Earth

This nighttime spectacular is one of the most impressive shows we have ever seen. The fireworks take place above the World Showcase Lagoon, accompanied by lasers, pyrotechnics, fountains and a giant globe.

The show's storyline is about the creation of earth, the troubles humanity has faced and uniting the world.

We recommend being in place a minimum of 30 minutes before the show begins for a decent view. There are many good viewing locations around the lake. Our favorite is between the UK and French pavilions.

You can also use a FastPass+ for a spot in a reserved viewing area, although we feel this is no better than most other locations around the lagoon.

Disney has announced that the show will be ending at the "end of summer 2019", when a new nighttime show will replace it.

Frozen Ever After Dessert Party:
This event takes place on select dates starting at 8:30pm and secures you a spot with a seat in a special viewing location, as well as desserts. Pricing is $79 for adults and $47 for children.

Illuminations Cruise:
For an exclusive viewing of the show, take an Illuminations Fireworks Cruise. After a short cruise in front of the hotels on Crescent Lake, your captain will park the boat under the bridge between the UK and French pavilions for a great view.

Boat rental starts at $300 (plus tax) for up to 8 people, with bigger boats also available. The price includes your captain, non-alcoholic refreshments and bagged snacks. This a much more private event than standing around the lagoon and for a large group is not bad value at all.

Disney's Hollywood Studios

Spanning 135 acres, Disney's Hollywood Studios was the third theme park to be built at the Walt Disney World Resort and opened in 1989.

The park is themed around Hollywood of the 1930s and 1940s. It hosted over 10.7 million guests in 2017, making it the ninth most visited theme park in the world, but the least visited park at the Walt Disney World Resort.

Throughout 2019, big changes are coming to the park, including the grand opening of a new land, Star Wars: Galaxy's Edge.

Hollywood Boulevard

Recreated to be like Hollywood with shops and restaurants, Hollywood Boulevard is the theme park equivalent of Main Street, U.S.A. in Magic Kingdom Park. It is the park's opening scene.

Mickey & Minnie's Runaway Railway - Opens in 2019

Opening in 2019, Mickey & Minnie's Runaway Railway will be a brand new attraction for Disney's Hollywood Studios.

Disney says the attraction will open in Summer 2019, although other details are sparse so far.

Here is how Disney describes it: "On the attraction, the fun begins when you see the premiere of a new cartoon short with Mickey and Minnie getting ready for a picnic. As they head out, they drive alongside a train and find out that the engineer is Goofy. Then, one magical moment lets you step into the movie and on Goofy's train for a wacky, wild ride.

Mickey & Minnie's Runaway Railway will put you inside the wacky and unpredictable world of a Mickey Mouse Cartoon Short where you're the star and anything can happen."

DINING:

The Hollywood Brown Derby - Table Service, DDP accepted, entrées are $16 to $29 at lunch and $19-$49 at dinner
The Trolley Car Café - Starbucks location serving drinks and snacks, DDP accepted, drinks and snacks are $3-$6 each

Sunset Boulevard

Sunset Boulevard contains many of the parks star attractions.

The Twilight Zone: Tower of Terror

The Tower of Terror transports you to another dimension dropping you 199 feet straight down – several times.

| FP Yes | 40" | Camera Yes | 7 mins | 20 to 60 mins |

Disney summarizes the ride nicely: "You are the passengers on a most uncommon elevator about to ascend into your very own episode of...*The Twilight Zone*. One stormy night long ago, five people stepped through the door of an elevator and into a nightmare. That door is opening once again, and this time it is opening for you."

The atmosphere inside the attraction is truly immersive and contains some of the best theming in the whole of the Walt Disney World Resort.

The pre-show is great and you will really feel the tension and anticipation even before you step foot on the actual ride vehicle itself. The Cast Members who work on this ride really add to the ambience with their creepy ways.

The on-ride effects before the actual drops are amazing, and it really does feel like your elevator is wildly out of control. The drops are fun but scary. The adrenaline is incredible, and it is definitely worth the visit.

Motors pull down the elevator faster than gravity, creating a weightless feeling. The Floridian version of this attraction is also unlike any other version of this ride around the world: the ride has a randomly selected sequence of drops each time.

If you do not visit the Tower of Terror during your time at the park, you will miss out on one of the best and most iconic rides at the Walt Disney World Resort.

A Fastpass+ reservation is recommended as the wait time can be long for this attraction. Do be aware, however, that by using Fastpass+ you will miss out on some details in the queue line.

Rock 'n' Roller coaster: Starring Aerosmith

Rock 'n' Roller coaster is a high-speed indoor roller coaster that is bound to get your heart racing.

During boarding, you will see Aerosmith getting ready for their show. Then, you'll hop aboard a Limo and take a high-speed ride through the Hollywood hills. You will go through 4.5Gs and reach speeds of 60mph in 3 seconds.

Yes | 48" | Yes | 5 mins | 40 to 85 mins

Each Limo is equipped with speakers all around your body, including around your head, and also has its own soundtrack for ultimate musical enjoyment. There are all kinds of inversions and loops and the ride is a lot of fun.

If you are not a roller coaster fan then this ride is probably not for you, but thrill enthusiasts are in for a treat!

A Single Rider line is available - it can save you a significant amount of time.

The attraction time stated above includes the pre-show.

Beauty and the Beast - Live on Stage

Yes | None | No | 25 mins | At set times

Step into the world of Belle and Gaston for a whirlwind version of the Disney classic 'Beauty and the Beast'.

This show is just like stepping into a Broadway performance with fantastic sets, costumes and props. It is well worth a viewing.

DINING:

Anaheim Produce - Snacks, DDP accepted, snacks are $2-$6
Catalina Eddie's - Quick Service, DDP accepted, entrées are $7.50-$11
Fairfax Fare - Quick Service, DDP accepted, entrées are $9.50-$13.50
Hollywood Scoops - Snacks, No DDP, ice creams are $5.50-$7
KRNR The Rock Station - Quick Service and Snacks, No DDP, entrées are $8.50-$10.50
Rosie's All-American Café - Quick Service, DDP accepted, entrées $10-$11.50
Sunshine Day Cafe - Quick Service, DDP accepted, entrées are $11-$12

Animation Courtyard

A good mixture of shows and walkthroughs await you in this area of the park.

Voyage of The Little Mermaid

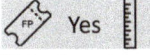   15 mins | At set times

This show is a mixture of live actors, puppets, and light, laser and rain effects retelling the story of The Little Mermaid.

Warning: The large Ursula puppet used during the show may scare some younger children.

Star Wars Launch Bay

This is a walkthrough exhibit featuring meet-and-greets with Star Wars characters, props from the movies and games to play.

It is a haven for Star Wars fans.

Disney Junior Dance Party

 Yes | Unknown

With catchy songs, puppets and a toddler friendly environment, Disney Junior is designed for the younger members of the family. At the time of writing the current incarnation of the attractions has closed. This new experience will open on December 22nd, 2018.

The official description is: "'Disney Junior Dance Party!' is a high-energy, live show experience that takes its inspiration from the most popular Disney Junior shows on TV, including "Mickey and the Roadster Racers," "Doc McStuffins," "The Lion Guard" and "Vampirina." The new "Disney Junior Dance Party!" is a musically infused, interactive concert, including live appearances from some of your favorite characters, fun music from Disney Junior and more."

Walt Disney Presents

No | None | No | 10-30 mins | None

This walkthrough exhibit details the fascinating life of Walt Disney, from his humble beginnings to his vision for the Walt Disney World Resort years later.

As you move along the timeline you can read the information, watch videos, and see models of the original Disneyland.

You can even see the newest additions to Disney theme parks around the world. It is a fascinating insight for aspiring Imagineers.

At the end of the exhibition you can either exit or you can watch an 18-minute short movie retelling Walt Disney's life story - all narrated by the man himself.

The theater is often used to show extended movie previews for upcoming Disney and Pixar productions. If this is the case during your visit, the movie preview will replace the movie about Walt Disney.

Disney's Hollywood Studios

Echo Lake

Star Tours - The Adventures Continue

This attraction is a must see for Star Wars fans, though if you know nothing about the franchise, the ride is still a lot of fun.

Once you have queued through the forest, you will enter an intergalactic space port. Here, you will see StarSpeeders, an alien air traffic control station, and robots hard at work to make your journey into space unforgettable.

Then, you board your vehicle for a tour of one of many planets – each time you experience the ride it is slightly different, with

FP	Height	Camera	Wait	Ride Length	Queue
Yes	40"	No	5 mins		15 to 45 mins

over 50 different scene combinations!

If you are prone to motion sickness Star Tours should be avoided, as this is a motion simulator experience. If you want a milder ride, ask to be sat in the front row as the movements here are less jarring.

Jedi Training – Trials of the Temple

FP		Camera		Wait		Showtimes
No	None	No		15 mins		At set times

For the younger adventurers, this is the chance to get up on stage and yield a lightsaber and battle the dark side.

Unfortunately for adults, only children can participate in the experience and take part in the show.

For those not participating, the show is still entertaining to watch.

Jedi Training takes place several times per day on the stage to the left of *Star Tours: The Adventures Continue*. Consult your park Times Guide for show times.

Indiana Jones Epic Stunt Spectacular

FP		Camera		Wait		Showtimes
Yes	None	No		30 mins		At set times

See Indi and his friends take on some death-defying stunts. Get ready for set changes, audience interaction and an explosive finale. A definite must watch for any day in the Studios.

For the First Time in Forever: A "Frozen" Celebration

Watch a retelling of the "Frozen" story with the historians of Arendelle. As the story evolves, the show becomes a sing-a-long every time a song comes on.

The show culminates with the arrival of Queen Anna and Princess Elsa, making for a stunning finale.

Yes | None | No | 25 mins | At set times

Dining:
50's Prime Time Café - Table Service, DDP accepted, entrées are $16-$26
Backlot Express - Snacks and Quick Service, DDP accepted, entrées are $8-$13.50
Dockside Diner - Quick Service, DDP accepted, entrées are $11-$11.50
Hollywood and Vine - Buffet Service, DDP accepted, breakfast is priced at $34-$39 per adult and $19-$23 per children, lunch is priced at $46-$55 for adults and $29-$37 for children, dinner is $47-$51 and $28-$33 respectively
Tune-In Lounge - Bar, No DDP, drinks are $5 and upwards

Commissary Lane

This area of the park does not contain any attractions, but includes a few dining locations.

Dining:
ABC Commissary - Quick Service and Snacks, DDP accepted, entrées are $10-$17
Sci-Fi Dine-In Theater Restaurant - Table Service, DDP accepted, entrées are $14-$27

Grand Avenue

Fans of the Kermit the Frog, Miss Piggy and others are in for a treat here.

Muppet Vision 3D

Yes | None | No | 30 mins | 15 mins or less

For Muppets fans, this is one attraction that should not be missed - a 3D experience with in-theater special effects, live action and more. This attraction is a good one to save for when you need a break from the heat, rain or walking, and often has low wait times.

Be prepared for a long, pre-show before the main 3D movie, which is very enjoyable. The show time listed includes the pre-show.

Dining:
Mama Melrose's Ristorante Italiano - Table Service, DDP accepted, entrées are $18-$33
Pizzerizzo - Quick Service, DDP accepted, entrées are $10-$11. Open seasonally.

Toy Story Land

Shrink down to the size of a toy to explore this world with Woody and his pals.

Toy Story Midway Mania

One of Walt Disney World's most popular attractions, Toy Story Midway Mania draws huge crowds of all ages; the result is long waits.

The ride is an interactive virtual shooting experience where each passenger in the car is given a gun to shoot at interactive screens with Toy Story characters. In some scenes you will shoot plates, in other balloons, with the aim to get the most points.

 Yes   None   No   5 mins 45 to 75 mins

It is great family fun but with an urge to win, you may find that your arm aches after riding.

Slinky Dog Dash

 Yes   38"   Yes   90 seconds   60 to 90 mintes

Slinky Dog invites you aboard his small but mighty family-friendly coaster.

Get great views of the surrounding area as you whiz across Toy Story Land on the Mega Coaster Play Kit that Andy's assembled.

This is a good starter coaster for kids - we recommend a FastPass+ reservation to ease the wait.

Alien Swirling Saucers

 Yes   32"   No   90 seconds   40 to 60 minutes

Hop inside a flying saucer powered by the Green Aliens from the Toy Story movies.

You will spin on a wild ride into space as you whip round each corner.

This attraction is very similar to the tea cups at Magic Kingdom but with bigger forces as you change direction. Fun for (almost) the whole family.

> **DINING:**
> **Woody's Lunch Box** - Quick Service, DDP accepted, entrées are $6-$8.50 at breakfast and $9-$13 at lunch and dinner.

Disney's Hollywood Studios

Star Wars: Galaxy's Edge

Star Wars: Galaxy's Edge is a brand new land spanning 14 acres which is set to open in late Fall 2019.

Based on a new planet in the Star Wars universe, Galaxy's Edge will house two new major attractions. In "Millennium Falcon: Smugglers Run" guests will take part in a secret mission. In "Star Wars: Rise of the Resistance" guests will be put face-to-face with the First Order.

Guests will be able to shop at Black Spire's marketplace,

Merchant Row and Smuggler's Row. Guests will also be able to meet characters.
Guests will be able to dine at the main restaurant - Oga's Cantina - as well as at Docking Bay 7 and Bantha Tracks and sample unique delights such as Blue Milk.

Live Entertainment

Citizens of Hollywood (Hollywood Boulevard) – Meet characters from Hollywood who present fun-filled shows during the day.

March of the First Order – Captain Phasma leads a squad of striking Stormtroopers.

Fireworks – This park hosts seasonal nightly firework and projection shows most of the year.

Fantasmic – Nighttime Spectacular

Fantasmic is Disney's Hollywood Studios' nighttime spectacular. The show combines character performances, water screen projections, fireworks, lasers, pyrotechnics and more. It should not be missed and appeals to all ages.

Arrive early to get the best seats in the 11,000-seat outdoor arena. If there are two performances on the same night, crowds will be smaller at the second one.

The Fastpass+ seating area

| FP Yes | None | 📷 No | ⏱ 30 mins | ⌛ At set times |

takes up about half of the stadium-style seating, so be sure to arrive early even with a Fastpass+ reservation as there is no guarantee of a great view.

Certain dining packages do entitle you to reserved seating.

At off-peak times, 'Fantasmic' only runs on select nights.

Disney's Animal Kingdom Park

Disney's Animal Kingdom Park is the Walt Disney World Resort's fourth and newest theme park. It opened on Earth Day (April 22) in 1998. Spanning 580 acres, it is the largest Disney park ever built. It is so big that you could fit all the other theme parks at Walt Disney World inside it and have room to spare.

Animal Kingdom is in our opinion the best themed of all the parks with a remarkable attention to detail. The park does not, however, have very many attractions and can be "seen" in less than a day. This is the sixth most visited park in the world, with 12.5 million visitors in 2017.

The entrance area of the park is called Oasis. It is a forest-like setting that immerses you in winding pathways and a stunning atmosphere from the moment you step in. The **Oasis Exhibits** are home to exotic animals housed along tropical garden pathways. For those wanting to eat in this area, Rainforest Café (Table Service, DDP accepted, entrées are $9-$15 at breakfast, and $17-$36 at lunch and dinner) is accessible from both inside and outside the park.

Discovery Island

This is the hub area of the park that holds the astounding Tree of Life, and leads to all the other lands of the park.

Tree of Life

Discover over 320 animals carved into this 145-foot tree, as you walk around it. The attention to detail is amazing – a true masterpiece.
At the Discovery Island trails, you can find otters, lemurs, flamingos, red kangaroos, storks, tortoises and more through these self-guided walks.

After sunset stick around for the tree of life's "awakenings" throughout the evening.

It's Tough to be a Bug

 Yes   None   No   9 mins   Less than 20 mins

The meanest and nastiest 3D show we have ever experienced. Be prepared to see how humans treat insects and then get a taste of your own medicine. Even when you think it is over, it is not! This attraction is likely to frighten adults, and terrify children. We do not recommend making Fastpass+ reservations as the queues for this show are usually very short.

Adventurers Outpost Meet and Greet

 Yes   Less than 30 mins

Get a photo with Mickey and Minnie in their Safari gear at this location. This is often one of the least crowded meet and greets featuring Mickey across all four parks.

DINING:
Creature Comforts - Starbucks, DDP accepted, drinks and snacks are $3-$5
Flame Tree Barbecue - Snacks and Quick Service, DDP accepted, entrées are $11-$19
Nomad Lounge - Bar and lounge, No DDP, appetizers are $9 to $17, drinks vary in price.
Pizzafari - Quick Service, DDP accepted, entrées are $10-$13.50
Tiffins - Signature Table Service, DDP accepted (2 Table Service credits required), entrées are $29-$53.

Winged Encounters – The Kingdom Takes Flight

This show takes place in front of the Tree of Life. It features different types of macaw and gives guests a chance to see them up close.

DinoLand U.S.A

Themed to a travelling carnival, DinoLand has several attractions listed below. As well as these there are also the Fossil Fun Games (carnival-style games – extra charge to play) and The Boneyard (a play area) to explore.

DINOSAUR

This is a scary, loud and turbulent journey through the past as you venture in search of an iguanodon dinosaur.

However, things may not go quite to plan.

This ride is a great thrill with an incredible ride vehicle, great storytelling and an immersive storyline.

It is a fun blast into the past but will likely scare younger visitors due to the darkness and the loud sound effects used throughout the attraction.

Yes | 40" | Yes | 3 mins | 20 to 45 min

TriceraTop Spin

No | None
No | 90 secs
Less than 15 mins

This is a spinning ride just like Dumbo at the Magic Kingdom, but themed to dinosaurs. It is fun, but nothing revolutionary, and usually has short queues. You can control how your dinosaur's height with a lever. Great for younger kids.

Primeval Whirl

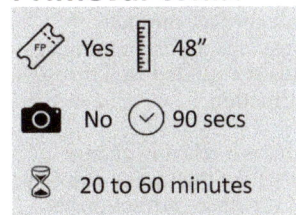

Yes | 48"
No | 90 secs
20 to 60 minutes

Primeval Whirl spins you round and round back in time to the prehistoric ages. The ride has some tight corners, short drops and is generally a good laugh. This may be too intense for a first roller coaster but it is a good mid-range coaster.

DINING:

Restaurantosaurus - Quick Service, DDP accepted, entrées are $9.50-$16

Africa

Travel to the African continent into a land filled with character and spice.

Kilimanjaro Safaris

Traverse the world's largest man-made savannah, spanning 110 acres on-board Kilimanjaro Safaris.

Join your guide for a ride on a safari style truck and get closer to the animals than you ever thought possible at a theme park.

Make sure you bring your camera as you may just get to see hippos, giraffes, monkeys, zebras, lions and more on this unpredictable adventure. It really is different every single time. The queue line for this attraction is tedious, so we recommend you make a FastPass+ reservation if possible.

FP: Yes | None | Camera: No | ✓ 20 mins | 30 to 60 min

Top Tip: The animals are most active in the morning, before it gets too hot, so try to get to this attraction early.

Gorilla Falls Exploration Trail

See gorillas, monkey, meerkats, birds and more in this self-guided walkthrough attraction.

This is a relaxing change from the long waits of many of the major attractions at this park. Here you can take the animals in at your own pace.

Wildlife Express Train

This is more a method of transport between Africa and Rafiki's Planet Watch than an actual attraction.

There are a few minor things to see along the way and it is a good place to rest for a few minutes or to seek shelter from the rain.

DINING:

Dawa Bar - Bar, No DDP, drinks are $7.50-$11
Harambe Fruit Market - Snacks, DDP accepted, fruit is $2-$6
Harambe Market - Quick Service, DDP accepted, entrées are $10-$13.50
Kusafiri Coffee Shop & Bakery - Snacks and Quick service, No DDP, entrées are $7-$11
Tamu Tamu Refreshments - Drinks and Desserts, DDP accepted, desserts are $5.50-$8
Tusker House Restaurant - Buffet, DDP accepted, the character breakfast is priced at $30-$38 per adult and $18-$23 per child. The non-character lunch and dinner buffet is priced at $37-$52 per adult, and $22-$31 per child

Rafiki's Planet Watch

To get to Rafiki's Planet Watch you will need to catch the Wildlife Express Train from the Africa area of the Park. This area will reopen in Spring 2019.

Habitat Habit!
Learn about how to protect endangered cotton-top tamarins in their natural homes. Guests also learn how to create animal habitats in their own homes.

Conservation Station
See the conservation efforts undertaken by The Walt Disney Company and take a behind the scenes look at how the animals are taken care of at Disney's Animal Kingdom, including a look at an examination room.

Affection Section
This is essentially a petting zoo with domesticated animals. Sometimes Cast Members will be present to tell you facts about the animals here.

"It All Started with a Mouse"

 No   20 mins

Conservation Station's "animal ambassadors" including sheep, parrots, porcupines, birds of prey and Kunekune pigs help tell stories and make appearances in, around, and even above the audience in this show.

Cast Members share natural history fun facts, conservation messages and inspiring calls-to-action.

After the show, you can meet some of the stars of the show and are encouraged to capture once-in-a-lifetime memories with plenty of photographs.

Asia

Asia contains some of the most exciting and popular attractions in the entire park, as well as some of the best theming.

Expedition Everest - Legend of the Forbidden Mountain

Expedition Everest is an incredible ride through the forbidden mountain where you might just get to see The Yeti in his natural habitat!

This is one attraction where you need to see the full queue line, as it is incredible - you even pass through a yeti museum while waiting!

Apart from the big drop you see outside the attraction there are no further big drops, but there are a few surprises in store.

| FP: Yes | 44" | Camera: Yes | 3 mins | 30 to 70 min |

The ride reaches maximum speeds of 50mph (80km/h). Expedition Everest is great fun and a very smooth coaster!

Ride it – this is one of Disney's best ever coasters!

Maharajah Jungle Trek

Take this self-guided walk and see komodo dragons, fruit bats, pythons, Bengal tigers, birds, deer, water buffalo and more.

This is an absolute must-visit for animal fans and it is the most exciting and interesting of the trails in our opinion, although this will depend on which animals you prefer to see.

Kali River Rapids

This fun raft water ride takes you through the forest. It makes sure that everyone gets at least a little bit wet - however, one or two people will come out soaked.

This attraction is particularly popular on hot summer days towards the middle of the day. We recommend making a Fastpass+ reservation as the queue line is slow.

Unfortunately, the ride is over before it hardly begins and we wish Disney had made it much longer. Nevertheless, it is fun while

Yes | 38" | No | 4 mins | 60 to 90 min

it lasts!

There are free lockers outside to the left of the attraction entrance for storing valuables. There is also a storage compartment in the center of the raft.

UP! A Great Bird Adventure

Yes | None | No | 25 mins | At set times

A bird show unlike any other with a fun storyline, a range of birds and some pretty impressive tricks, as well as Doug and Russell from the hit-movie 'Up!'.

The seating area is covered, providing shade and shelter, but it is not air-conditioned.

This show is presented up to 5 times daily in the Asia area of the park.

DINING:

Thirsty River Bar and Trek Snacks - Bar and Snacks, No DDP, snacks are $3-$5
Yak & Yeti Local Food Cafes - Quick Service, DDP accepted, entrées are $9-$10 at breakfast and $11-$15 at lunch and dinner
Yak & Yeti Quality Beverages Lounge - Bar and snacks, No DDP, entrées are $10-$15 and drinks are $3-$10
Yak & Yeti Restaurant - Table Service, DDP accepted, entrées are $18-$29

Disney's Animal Kingdom Park

Pandora: World of Avatar

Inspired by the highest grossing film of all time, Pandora: World of Avatar is Animal Kingdom's newest area. It opened in Summer 2017,

AVATAR: Flight of Passage

Flight of Passage is Animal Kingdom's most popular attraction, and one of the most technologically advanced attractions Disney has ever created.

This motion simulator has you sitting on the back of a Banshee (flying creature) and then soaring around the world of Pandora - around mountains, water and scenery.

Through the 3D goggles, high-definition video and all sorts of clever sensory techniques, you are transported to another world - this is an immersive experience not to miss.

Yes | 44" | No | 4.5 mins | 120 to 180 mins

Guests who are scared of heights or simulated drops may wish to avoid this ride.

The ride vehicles are individual motorbike-style restraints and may not accommodate larger guests.

Expect long wait times throughout the whole day - head here as soon as the park opens if you don't manage to get a Fastpass+ reservation. On the busiest of days, expect to see a wait of up to 4 hours.

Na'vi River Journey

Na'vi River Journey is Pandora's more family-friendly attraction. Here you sit on a riverboat and calmly pass the nighttime jungle scenery of Pandora.

You'll see creatures, bioilluminescent plants and other forest life around you.

The most impressive part of the ride is when you see a shaman beating musical drums - this is an incredibly lifelike animatronic

Yes | None | No | 4.5 mins | 60 to 90 min

(pictured) that has to be seen to be believed.

There are no moments that should frighten children.

DINING:
Pongo Pongu - Bar and Snacks, DDP accepted, snacks are $5-11 and drinks are $6-$19
Satu'li Canteen - Quick Service, DDP accepted, entrées are $11-$16

Live Shows

Festival of the Lion King

'The Festival of The Lion King' is our favorite show at the Walt Disney World Resort and a true celebration of the essence of The Lion King movies.

The show does not follow a movie storyline, but instead includes the best songs interpreted by professionals in an African-inspired theme. This is a definite must-do. This show is presented in the Africa area of the park.

FP: Yes | None | No | 30 mins | At set times

Finding Nemo: The Musical

This is a Broadway-style show that has convinced us that Finding Nemo should have been a musical all along!

The show has great sets, costumes and actors. Take the time to see this family-friendly production.

This show is located in Dinoland USA area of the park.

FP: Yes | None | No | 40 mins | At set times

Rivers of Light - Nighttime Spectacular

This nighttime spectacular features live music, floating lanterns, water screens and swirling animal imagery bringing a show to Discovery River that delights guests and truly caps off their day.

Dedicated viewing and seating areas are available in Asia and Dinoland USA.

FP: Yes | None | No | 16 mins | At set times

Chapter Eleven | MyMagic+

MyMagic+

MyMagic+ is Disney's tool for planning a seamless vacation. MyMagic+ is made up of three main components: My Disney Experience, FastPass+ (covered in the next chapter) and MagicBands.

My Disney Experience

This is a website and a mobile app that allow you to:
• Get you all the information you need in one place; plan as much, or as little, as you want.
• Make dining, FastPass+ and other reservations in advance
• See your in-park photos, including ride photos
• Purchase Memory Maker to receive access to all photos and videos from your vacation
• Purchase park tickets
• See park maps
• See wait times for attractions and selected meet and greet experiences

MagicBands

Disney resort hotel guests are entitled to use an RFID-enabled MagicBand that ties together all the features of MyMagic+.

The MagicBand is worn on your wrist throughout your vacation. It allows you to check-in for Disney's Magical Express, open your Disney resort hotel room door, pay for food and merchandise, use Disney Dining Plans, make and use FastPass+ reservations, use Disney's Photopass service, have automatic on-ride photos, and enter the theme parks and water parks.

MagicBands are shipped 10 to 30 days before arrival to US addresses, or to the resort if your reservation is made within 10 days of arrival. International visitors receive their MagicBand at hotel check-in.

If you are not staying at a Disney resort hotel, you can purchase a MagicBand for $14.99 from Walt Disney World Resort stores, although MagicBands do not do very much for non-Disney hotel guests except allow you to tap into the parks and attractions instead of using your park ticket, and linking photos and videos to PhotoPass and Memory Maker accounts.

MagicBands & special events: Throughout the year, in-park events take place outside of regular park hours, and require a separate 'hard ticket' such as Magic Kingdom's Halloween and Christmas parties. You can seamlessly use your MagicBands during events.

You can link your separate 'hard ticket' admission ticket to your "My Disney Experience" account by entering the ticket number on the website or the app. If you bought the ticket on the Disney website, you may find that it is already automatically linked. This allows you to enter the park with a MagicBand instead of using a paper ticket.

You will be given a physical 'event wristband' for special events at the park entrance if you enter after a certain time. Guests who enter the park before this time will need to present themselves at a designated location inside the park to pick up an event wristband. You must wear an event wristband during special events, as well as optionally wearing a MagicBand.

Fastpass+ is not available during hard ticketed events. Only stand-by queue lines are used. Touch to Pay, PhotoPass and Memory Maker work as normal.

FastPass+

The Walt Disney World Resort offers a time-saving system, called FastPass+ that allows you to make reservations for rides, shows, parades, meet and greets and more. These reservations allow you access to attractions with little to no wait, skipping the regular queue line. This service is available on certain attractions across all four theme parks – a list of these attractions is available later.

Every theme park entry ticket and annual pass includes the free Fastpass+ service. You do not pay for Fastpass+ as it is always included in your admission price.

Disney's FastPass+ allows you to reserve spots on rides before you've even reached the theme parks. When you can begin making FastPass+ reservations depends on whether you are stay on-site or off-site.

Staying On-Site:
If you are staying at a Walt Disney World Resort hotel, *60 days* before the beginning of your trip you will be able to make FastPass+ reservations for up to three attractions, shows or other experiences for each day of your vacation online at the My Disney Experience website (disneyworld. Disney.go.com/plan/) or via the My Disney Experience app.

Staying Off-Site:
If you are not staying at a Walt Disney World Resort hotel, you can make FastPass+ reservations up to *30 days* in advance, provided you have pre-purchased your tickets before your visit begins and linked these on the My Disney Experience website (you will need to register for a free account).

Whether you are staying on-site or off-site, during your visit you can add and change FastPass+ reservations by going to a FastPass+ kiosk or by using the My Disney Experience app.

More details:
In both instances, you will be able to make FastPass+ reservations starting at 7:00am Eastern Time either 30 or 60 days before your vacation. If you are not logged in at 7:00am EST, there is a good chance you will miss some of the most popular FastPass+ experiences such as AVATAR: Flight of Passage, Seven Dwarfs Mine Train, Frozen Ever After and Slinky Dog Dash.

If staying at a Disney hotel, you can make FastPass+ reservations for the length of your stay at 7:00am EST, not just the first day. Guests staying off-site will need to visit the website daily at 7:00am EST 30 days before each day of their vacation.

SPECIAL EXCEPTIONS:
One Day Ticket with Pre-Selected FastPasses - This will not apply to the vast majority of readers (if any at all) as we doubt you have purchased this guide for a 1-Day visit. This ticket is more aimed at anyone who turns up at the park having done no research. The ticket is the same price as a regular 1-Day ticket and includes 3 pre-selected FastPass+ reservations.

Disney Club Level Extra FastPass+ - If you are booked into club level at a Disney resort hotel, Disney allows you an extra 3 FastPass+ reservations per day, plus reserved seating at one nighttime show - for an additional $50 per person per day. These FastPass+ reservations can be made 90 days before arrival. This is not good value for money in our opinion, but if you have the money to spare and very limited time, this may make sense. If not, simply follow the tips in this chapter for which FastPass+ reservations you should make and how.

How to make FastPass+ reservations

The steps to make FastPass+ reservations are the same on the My Disney Experience website, the smartphone app, or the in-park FastPass+ kiosks.

Before following this process remember to be signed in and have your park tickets and if applicable, a Disney hotel reservation, linked on the website or app (at an in-park kiosk you can simply touch your MagicBand).

• Click add Fastpass. Select the names of the people you will be making FastPass+ reservations for.
• Select the date and which park you will be in for the given day.
• Select a time for your reservations - morning, afternoon, evening or a custom time.
 o At Magic Kingdom, you can choose any three experiences.
 o At Epcot, Animal Kingdom and Disney's Hollywood Studios you must choose a certain number of attractions from Tier 1 and another number of attractions from Tier 2. There is more information on these Tiers later.
• You will be presented with a list of possible 1-hour time slots for attractions if FastPass+ reservations are still available – usually you will be presented with up to three different time slots.

There may also be an option to see other times. If not, you can make a reservation and modify the time later.
• Once you have reserved one attraction, you can then make another - up to three advanced FastPass+ reservations can be made per day for one theme park.

At the park when it is time to use your FastPass+ reservation, simply show up to the ride, show or firework viewing area and tap your MagicBand or park ticket on the Mickey head receiver by the FastPass+ entrance to be granted access by a Cast Member.

FastPass+ reservation logistics

• You are limited to making up to three FastPass+ reservations in advance at one park per day. If you arrive in the park spontaneously, you can make up to three reservations in the same park when you arrive by visiting one of the Fastpass+ kiosks or via the My Disney Experience app.
• Epcot, Animal Kingdom and Hollywood Studios offer a tiered system for your first three bookings - this limits which rides you can reserve in advance from each group. After you have used all 3 initial FastPass+ reservations, you are able to make "additional" FastPass+ reservations for any attraction, regardless of its tier.
• You can only make one advanced FastPass+ reservation per ride or experience per day. This means that if you wanted to ride Big Thunder Mountain more than once, you can only use 1 of your 3 advanced FastPass+ experiences for this. Once all three advanced FastPass+ experiences have been used, you can make "additional" Fastpass+ reservations for any attraction, including rides you have already ridden on that day.
• If one of your first three Fastpass+ reservations is made towards the end of the park's operating day, you will not be able to make "additional" Fastpass+ experiences until you have

Fastpass+

used all of your advanced reservations.
- Once you have *used* one of your Fastpass+ reservations, you may make or change reservations for any park - not just the one you are in.

How to make additional FastPass+ reservations:

Once you have used at least one of your advanced FastPass+ reservations, you can then make "additional" in-park reservations. These "additional reservations" can be made via the My Disney Experience app or at the in-park FastPass+ kiosks.

For these "additional" reservations, you can reserve any ride, show or viewing spot at any of the theme parks provided there are free FastPass+ reservation slots – you do not have be present inside the park you want to use the FastPass+ in when making the reservation.

For example, if you have spent the morning at Magic Kingdom Park using your pre-booked FastPass+ reservations and wanted to book a FastPass+ attraction at Epcot, you can do this even while still at Magic Kingdom. Just be sure to allow enough travel time.

You can only make one

of these "additional" reservations at a time. Once your "additional" FastPass+ reservation has been used, you can make another FastPass+ reservation. You can repeat this as many times as you want until the end of the day.

Top Tip 1: If you have not already done this on the My Disney Experience website or app, ask a Cast Member to link all your family's park tickets so you can select FastPass+ experiences for all your family at once. This will save you a lot of time, and you can still make individual changes. You can find this option quite easily – just click the "Add another guest to your travel party" option when making your FastPass+ reservations.

Top Tip 2: When you book a particular FastPass+ you sometimes get a "surprise" FastPass+ reservation for another attraction. These try to divert you to attractions that have shorter wait times. If you do not want a certain "surprise" FastPass+ reservation, you can change it for another attraction.

Fastpass+

List of Fastpass+ Experiences:

Magic Kingdom:
- Big Thunder Mountain Railroad
- Buzz Lightyear's Space Ranger Spin
- Dumbo the Flying Elephant
- Enchanted Tales with Belle
- Haunted Mansion
- "it's a small world"
- Jungle Cruise
- Mad Tea Party
- Meet Ariel at Ariel's Grotto
- Meet Cinderella and a Visiting Princess at Princess Fairytale Hall
- Meet Rapunzel and a Visiting Princess at Princess Fairytale Hall
- Meet Mickey Mouse at Town Square Theater
- Meet Tinker Bell at Town Square Theater
- Mickey's Philharmagic
- Monsters Inc. Laugh Floor
- Peter Pan's Flight
- Pirates of the Caribbean
- Seven Dwarfs Mine Train
- Space Mountain
- Splash Mountain
- The Barnstormer
- The Magic Carpets of Aladdin
- The Many Adventures of Winnie the Pooh
- Tomorrowland Speedway
- Under the Sea: Journey of the Little Mermaid

At Magic Kingdom you can choose any combination of experiences. At Epcot, Animal Kingdom and Hollywood Studios you choose 1 attraction from Tier 1 and 2 from Tier 2.

Disney's Animal Kingdom Park:
Tier 1 (Choose one attraction):
- AVATAR: Flight of Passage
- Na'vi River Journey

Tier 2 (Choose two attractions):
- Adventurers Outpost
- Dinosaur
- Expedition Everest
- Festival of the Lion King
- Finding Nemo: The Musical
- It's Tough to be a Bug
- Kali River Rapids
- Kilimanjaro Safaris
- Primeval Whirl
- Rivers of Light
- Up! A Great Bird Adventure

Disney's Hollywood Studios:
Tier 1 (Choose one attraction):
- Alien Swirling Saucers
- Slinky Dog Dash
- Toy Story Midway Mania

Tier 2 (Choose two attractions):
- Beauty and the Beast – Live on Stage
- Rock 'n' Roller Coaster Starring Aerosmith
- Fantasmic!
- Frozen Sing-Along Celebration
- Indiana Jones Epic Stunt Spectacular!
- Muppet*Vision 3D
- Star Tours - The Adventures Continue
- The Twilight Zone: Tower of Terror
- Voyage of the Little Mermaid

Epcot:
Tier 1 (Choose one attraction):
- Frozen Ever After
- Illuminations: Reflections of Earth
- Soarin'
- Test Track

Tier 2 (Choose two attractions):
- Disney & Pixar Short Film Festival
- Epcot Character Spot
- Journey into Imagination with Figment
- Living with the Land
- Mission: SPACE
- Spaceship Earth
- The Seas with Nemo & Friends
- Turtle Talk with Crush

More Important Information

- With the tiered group system, you cannot make advanced Fastpass+ reservations for two Tier 1 attractions on the same day. To get around this, make a reservation for one of the attractions in Tier 1, and using the standby line for another.

Alternatively, once you have used your three advanced FastPass+ experiences, you can make a reservation for any attraction, regardless of its tier, subject to availability.

The likelihood of their being FastPass+ reservations available at these attractions "top tier" attractions is very low, however. Later in this section, we also cover the more "valuable" FastPass+ reservations.

- Cast Members will not allow you to use a FastPass+ reservation before or after your reservation time. However, there is a 5-minute leeway before and 15 minutes after your slot. The exception is if an attraction breaks down, in which case FastPass+ reservations are valid all day. If you encounter any other problem that makes you late (such as a dining reservation), it is still worth speaking to the Cast Member at the ride entrance, as they are able to override the system.
- Some rides like The Twilight Zone: Tower of Terror and Rock 'n' Roller coaster have a pre-show video that you will have to watch, even with a FastPass+ reservation. This can add up to 15 minutes of queuing. Waits in the Soarin' FastPass+ line are also often longer than 20 minutes, as are those for AVATAR: Flight of Passage and Slinky Dog Dash.
- You can make separate FastPass+ reservations for every member of your party. This means that two people in your party can go and ride Big Thunder Mountain, while the others ride "it's a small world". Or you can all do the same thing – it is up to you.
- If you do not book your experiences in advance, you can still make day-of-visit reservations in the parks with FastPass+ kiosks or with the My Disney Experience smartphone app. We strongly recommend making reservations in advance, however, as on-the-day availability is very limited.
- Free Wi-Fi is available throughout the parks, Disney Springs and the Disney resort hotels to enable you to access My Disney Experience almost anywhere on Disney property.
- You can change a FastPass+ reservation if you have not yet used it – including changing its time, or swapping it for a different attraction.
- Until you use your first FastPass+ reservation on each day, you can still change all your reservations – including the theme park you will be using Fastpass+ for. So, if you arrive at a park with FastPass+ reservations and notice the waits are low for everything, do not use any of your FastPass+ reservations and swap them for a different park (subject to availability).
- Annual Passholders with a MagicBand can make FastPass+ reservations up to 30 days in advance, with 7 days of reservations allowed in any 30-day period. Annual Passholders do not have to be staying at a Disney hotel to take advantage of this.

What rides should I make FastPass+ reservations for?

Making FastPass+ reservations for certain attractions will save you a lot of time whereas others do not really need a reservation, as they often have short wait times. Here are FastPass+ reservations from the most to the least important - the most important are at the top of the list.

Magic Kingdom:
1. Seven Dwarf's Mine Train
2. Peter Pan's Flight
3. Space Mountain
4. Splash Mountain
5. Big Thunder Mountain Railroad
6. Enchanted Tales with Belle
7. Buzz Lightyear's Space Ranger Spin
8. Jungle Cruise
9. Haunted Mansion
10. The Many Adventures of Winnie the Pooh
11. Under the Sea: Journey of the Little Mermaid

EPCOT
1. Frozen Ever After
2. Soarin'
3. Test Track
4. Mission: SPACE

Disney's Hollywood Studios:
1. Slinky Dog Dash
2. Toy Story: Midway Mania
3. Rock 'n' Roller coaster: Starring Aerosmith
4. The Twilight Zone: Tower of Terror
5. Alien Swirling Saucers
6. Fantasmic!
7. Star Tours: The Adventures Continue

(Once Star Wars: Galaxy's Edge opens, we expect both attractions to be extremely popular and would put those at the top of the list. Mickey & Minnie's Runaway Railway will also likely be popular when it opens)

Disney's Animal Kingdom:
1. AVATAR: Flight of Passage
2. Expedition Everest
3. Kali River Rapids
4. Primeval Whirl
5. Kilimanjaro Safaris
6. Na'vi River Journey
7. Dinosaur
8. Adventurers Outpost: Meet and Greet

How to get those 'hard to get' Fastpasses

Log into My Disney Experience's (the app or website) FastPass+ page at exactly 7:00am Eastern Time, either 30 days before your trip (for non-Disney hotel guests) or 60 days before (for Disney hotel guests). You must be logged in this early for the most popular Fastpasses.

Even being logged in this far in advance, some FastPass+ reservations are very difficult to get – Frozen Ever After, Seven Dwarfs Mine Train, Slinky Dog, AVATAR: Flight of Passage and Toy Story Midway Mania are some good examples.

If you cannot get a FastPass+ reservation for a particular attraction, there is a solution. This strategy works both with advance FastPass+ reservations and those made on the day itself. It works on the website, mobile apps and in-park FastPass+ kiosks.

Understanding the system:
My Disney Experience looks for FastPass+ reservation times for all members in your party at the same time. So, if you want to visit Toy Story Mania and there are 4 people in your party, the system will look for a time slot for 4 people to enter together. If it cannot find a slot for 4 people, it will say there is no availability.

However, if you look for a slot for only 2 or 3 people, you may find availability. This means that you should look for a reservation for a smaller number of people than are in your party first. Then, once you have confirmed that reservation, look for another reservation for the remaining members of your party.

With some luck, the reservation times will overlap and you can all ride together! If they do not overlap, take the FastPass+ reservations anyway and try to modify the times later.

Chapter Thirteen | Park Touring Strategies

Park Touring Strategies

This chapter is intended to help you tour the parks and reduce your time waiting in queue lines. It is not a complete touring plan but instead strategies of which attractions should be done when.

Before we begin...

It is imperative that you be at the park turnstiles at least 30 minutes before the official opening time of each park, with your park ticket in hand, in order to make the most of these park touring strategies.

Top Tip 1: The theme parks regularly allow guests in up to 30 minutes before the published opening time, with select attractions open. Being at the park entrance early lets you take advantage of this 'secret early entry'.

Top Tip 2: As long as you are in a queue line by the closing time of a theme park, you will be able to experience the attraction, no matter how long the wait is. E.g. It is 9:59pm and the Magic Kingdom closes at 10:00pm and the wait time for Space Mountain is 25 minutes. Get in line now and you will still be allowed to ride even though you will ride after the official park closing time.

Top Tip 3: If you wish to ride one of the top attractions without a FastPass+ reservation, do not attempt this on a day with morning Extra Magic Hours as the parks are much busier than they would otherwise be. You should especially avoid these days if you do not have access to the EMHs as the park will be busy before you even enter.

Epcot

Frozen Ever After is Epcot's newest ride and with the popularity of Frozen as strong as ever, this ride usually has the longest wait in the park. You should make a FastPass+ reservation for this attraction in advance. If you cannot get a reservation, then leave this attraction until the end of the day.

Test Track is the second most popular attraction in this park – it is on the left hand side of the park. You should go here first as soon as the park opens.

Next cross to the right-hand side of the park and head over to *Soarin'*, and finally cross the park again to ride *Mission: Space*. This will involve a lot of going back and forth but it is the best use of your time.

Once you have done these three rides, all the major long-lined rides are done - with the exception of *Frozen Ever After*!

Alternatively, if you are happy splitting up your group, do *Soarin'* first followed by *Test Track* in the Single Rider line.

The lines for *Spaceship Earth* (inside the giant 'golf ball') are huge at the start of the day but in the afternoon this attraction is always a walk-on with no wait, so ride it later in the day.

Epcot Character Spot, the *Magic Eye Theater*, *Ellen's Energy Adventure*, *The Seas*

with Nemo and Friends, *Journey into Imagination with Figment* and *Living with the Land* very rarely have waits of over 20 minutes, with most of these being walk-ons all day long. If the wait is longer than this for any of these attractions, then return later in the day.

Park Touring Strategies

Magic Kingdom

Big Thrills:
FastPass+ reservations should be made for *Peter Pan's Flight, Seven Dwarfs Mine Train* and *Jungle Cruise*.

If you cannot get an advanced FastPass+ reservation for *Seven Dwarfs Mine Train*, go there first and then follow the next step.

If you do have a *Seven Dwarfs Mine Train* reservation, the first thing you should do at park opening is hit the three 'mountains' in the following order: *Space Mountain, Big Thunder Mountain* and *Splash Mountain*. You can often do all of these within the first hour of park opening. Later in the day, these will often have waits of two hours *each* on peak days.

After 9:30pm (assuming *Happily Ever After* is showing at 10:00pm), most rides will have a line of 10 minutes of less – *Under the Sea, Buzz Lightyear* and *Winnie the Pooh* are three examples of rides which have waits of about

60 minutes for most of the day but are walk-ons in the evening. The same also applies to *Peter Pan's Flight* which does not usually have a wait of more than 20 minutes this late at night (despite what may be posted as the wait time).

At shows such as *Carousel of Progress, Monsters Inc. Laugh Floor, Mickey's Philharmagic, Country Bear Jamboree* and *Enchanted Tiki Room*, you should never wait more than 15 minutes. If the wait time is longer, come back later.

Kids' Favorites:
Make your FastPass+ reservations for the *Seven Dwarfs Mine Train, Jungle Cruise* and *Enchanted Tales with Belle*. Those hoping to meet the princesses in *Fairytale Hall* should make

this their most important Fastpass+ reservation (substituting *Jungle Cruise* above). Do check the height requirement for *Seven Dwarfs Mine Train*.

At park opening, you will want to head to *Peter Pan's Flight first*, followed by *The Barnstormer* (a small roller coaster), *Winnie the Pooh* and *Under the Sea*. You can usually do these four rides within the first 60 minutes of the park opening provided you keep up the pace. Work your way around Fantasyland.

The wait time for *"it's a small word"* rarely exceeds 25 minutes so you can do that at any point of the day; the same applies to all of the shows.

Disney's Hollywood Studios

Assuming you have a FastPass+ reservation for *Slinky Dog*, at park opening the ride you absolutely have to ride first is *Toy Story Midway Mania*. If you are not in the queue line within the first 20 to 25 minutes of the park opening, be prepared to wait 45 to 75 minutes at any other time.

If you do not have a FastPass+ reservation for *Slinky Dog*, then head there first. Make a FastPass+ reservation for *Toy Story Midway Mania*.

Try to avoid visiting this park on a day when it has morning Extra Magic Hours if you are not staying at a Disney hotel, as that will quickly mess up your ability to do your first ride quickly in the morning.

After *Midway Mania*, ride *Rock 'n' Roller coaster and Tower of Terror*, in that order.

Most of the other attractions are shows – be there at least 20 minutes before they start for a good seat.

Voyage of the Little Mermaid sometimes has waits of over 30 minutes. If this is the case, come back later. The show runs continuously throughout the day – you should not have to wait any longer than until the next show starts (every 20 minutes or so).

Star Tours' wait time fluctuates throughout the day, but you should not have to wait for more than 20 minutes for this attraction.

One Star Wars: Galaxy's Edge opens in late 2019, we recommend heading there first making a FastPass+ reservation for one of the rides and going straight for the other when the park opens. We would then ride *Rock 'n' Roller coaster and Tower of Terror*, and see the shows and leave Toy Story Land's attractions for the end of the day.

Disney's Animal Kingdom

Ideally you should have a FastPass+ reservation for *AVATAR: Flight of Passage*. If so, head for *Na'vi River Journey*. If not, head straight to *AVATAR: Flight of Passage* at park opening - exceptionally you must be at the park gates at least 1 hour before opening (not 30 minutes like the other parks). Then follow the plan below - save *Na'vi River Journey* for the very end of the day.

Expedition Everest should be your next port of call, followed by *Kilimanjaro Safaris* (the animals are most active in the morning!) and then *Kali River Rapids*.

On very hot days, queues for *Kali River Rapids* get very long from 11:00am onwards. If this is a priority for you, make a FastPass+ reservation.

The wait time for *DINOSAUR* fluctuates throughout the day but you should not wait for longer than 20 minutes. If the wait is longer, come back later – or do it at park closing.

Primeval Whirl often has one of the longest and most tedious queues throughout the day. Avoid the queue by making a FastPass+ reservation.

Everything else is a show; simply turn up 15 to 20 minutes before they are scheduled to start for a good seat.

Blizzard Beach Water Park

One of Disney's two water parks, Blizzard Beach has a storyline unlike any other. Disney says that a freak snowstorm came to Florida leading to the creation of the state's first ski resort. The snow then started to melt leading to "the most slushy, slippery, exhilarating water park anywhere!"

Disney Water Park Basics

- Coolers are allowed in the water parks. Glass and alcohol are not permitted.
- Mats, inner tubes and floatation devices are provided at no charge.
- Seating and cabanas can be reserved for a charge.
- Several locations offer hair wraps and temporary tattoos.
- Parks are non-smoking except in certain areas.
- One of the two water parks closes between November and February. This is then followed by the closure of the other water park. From March to October, both parks are open daily.
- Parks may close due to weather issues – no refunds are given; get a hand stamp to return later in the day.
- Life jackets rentals are complimentary – a refundable deposit is required.
- Changing rooms and showers are available.
- Consider the Water Parks Annual Pass that includes unlimited admission to both water parks for one year. Pricing is about $138.45 with tax per person.
- Unlimited admission to the Disney water parks is included with the most expensive Walt Disney World Annual Pass.
- Children of diaper age must wear tight-fitting rubber pants over their diapers, or special swimming diapers at the water park.
- Swimsuits with rivets, buckles or exposed metal are not allowed on the slides.
- Children under 10 years old must be accompanied by an adult at all times.
- A park-specific mug can be purchased for $11.99 (plus tax) and can be refilled all day at various locations throughout the park.
- Parking at the water parks is free.

Top water park tips

- Bring something to wear on your feet as the walkways become very hot!
- Arrive early to get a lounger with shade, or alternatively arrive in the afternoon when crowds will have thinned out.
- Buy a disposable waterproof camera for unforgettable pictures.
- If there is a thunderstorm, you will be asked to leave the water and all rides will temporarily shut down. Brave it out, as thunderstorms are usually brief, and you will find a much emptier park when the attractions re-open.

Blizzard Beach Basics

- Entry into Blizzard Beach is priced at $69.03 for adults and $62.84 for children, including tax.
- At Beach Haus you can find beach apparel, souvenirs, sundries and film. You can also view and purchase Photopass photos here.
- Lockers are available to rent at Snowless Joe's - $10 for a small locker and $15 for a large locker. Lockers can also be rented at other locations around the park.
- Towels can be rented at Snowless Joe's for $2 each.
- Lost children are brought to Snowless Joe's.
- Volleyball nets are available at the park.
- Sometimes Blizzard Beach's character mascot Ice Gator makes appearances for photos in the village area of the park – check with Guest Relations for timings.

Reserved Seating and Cabanas

There are two areas that can be reserved – both require wristbands to access, given when checking in at the park:

- **Polar Patios** – There are 4 cabanas available to rent in this area accommodating up to 6 guests each. The cost varies between $225 and $340 plus tax, depending on the season. Additional guests can be added for $25 each. Cabanas include a one-day refillable drinks mug for each person, a cooler with ice and bottled water, lounge furniture, rental towels, private lockers and waiter service. Reservations can be made up to 180 days in advance by calling 407-WDW-PLAY. On the day reservations are subject to availability.

- **Lottawatta Lodge Picnic Umbrellas** – This area includes 2 lounge chairs, an umbrella, small table and two towels. Pricing is between $40 and $60 plus tax for 2 to 4 people. Reservations can be made up to 180 days in advance by calling 407-WDW-PLAY. On the day reservations are subject to availability.

Attractions

Green Slope

Summit Plummet – Guests must be 48 inches (1.22m) or taller to ride. This is the park's premier attraction and at 120-feet tall is one of the tallest and fastest free-fall slides in the world. You will see it as you approach the park with riders braving speeds of up to 60 miles per hour!

Teamboat Springs – This ride is yet another record breaker, being the longest "family white-water raft ride" in the world at 1,400 feet (427 m) in length. Guests board a big blue raft with handles and room for four to six people – and it is a wild, downhill ride from there! Infants may not ride.

Slush Gusher – Guests must be 48 inches (1.22m) or taller to ride. This body slide has you reaching speeds of up to 35 mph, as you follow its 250-foot long course. Due to its layout, it is one of only a few water slides where you really get some "air time".

Red Slope

Runoff Rapids – These are a series of 600-foot inner tube slides – two are open-air and one is enclosed. There are multiple slides but you cannot race as all the slides are different lengths. Access to this attraction is via stairs only.

Purple Slope

Downhill Double Dipper – Guests must be 48 inches (1.22m) or taller to ride. A racing slide where guests board inner tubes, push their tubes out and wait at the automated gates. When everyone is lined up, there is a countdown and the gates all open at once. At the bottom of the hill, each slide has its own timer to see who won the race. Great fun for competitive types.

Snow Stormers – This is a mat slide where guests lie on their stomachs on a toboggan style mat. There are 3 flumes and each is 350-feet long.

Toboggan Racers – This is the most competitive-looking of all the slides at Blizzard Beach. There are 8 identical lanes, each 250 feet long. Guests line up on their mats and stomachs and wait

for the signal, then push off, race down the slopes and see who reaches the furthest, the fastest.

Ground Level

The Chairlift – This is a one-way ride from Ground Level to the summit of Mount Gushmore where all the green slides are located. Guests with disabilities may use the chairlift for return trips. Each wooden bench carries up to 3 people and the ride lasts about 4 minutes. There is an accessible Gondola too. Guests must be at least 32 inches tall to ride. To ride alone guests must be at least 48 inches (1.22m) tall.

Cross Country Creek – This is a lazy river that goes all the way round the park, totalling 3000 feet. There are seven entrances and exits and floating devices (inner tubes) are available at each of them. The journey takes 20 to 30 minutes for a full loop. Beware of the icy cave!

Melt-Away Bay – A one acre wave pool with constant short bobbing waves.

Tike's Peak – This area features kiddie versions of some of the bigger slides. There is also a fountain play area themed to a snow castle and picnic benches. Guests must be 48 inches (1.22m) tall or shorter.

Ski Patrol Training Camp – This area is split into several attractions: Cool Runners is an inner tube area, Leisure Pool has icebergs which

kids under 12 can walk across, Freezin' Pipe Springs is a short body slide and Fahrenheit Drops is a T-bar drop attraction that drops guests that are under five feet (1.52 m) tall into 8.5 feet (2.6 m) deep water – being able to swim or using a floatation device is essential.

DINING:

Avalunch - Snacks and Quick Service, DDP accepted, entrées are $10-$11
Cooling Hut - Sandwiches, snacks, desserts and drinks, DDP accepted, prices are $4-$11
Frostbite Freddy's Frozen Freshments - Snacks, No DDP, entrées and desserts are $4.50-$12
I.C. Expeditions - Snacks, No DDP, snacks are $4.50-$14
Lottawatta Lodge - Snacks and Quick Service, DDP accepted, entrées are $8.50-$11
Mini Donuts - Snacks, donuts and drinks, No DDP, donuts are $5-$10
Polar Pub - Bar, serves alcoholic and non-alcoholic drinks, No DDP, $3-$11
Warming Hut - Snacks and Quick Service sandwiches, DDP accepted, entrées are $9-$11

Chapter Fifteen | Typhoon Lagoon Water Park

Typhoon Lagoon Water Park

Typhoon Lagoon Water Park is home to the world's largest outdoor wave pool. The story goes that Typhoon Lagoon was once a tropical paradise when a typhoon came through and wreaked havoc, including "Miss Tilly", a boat that was flung onto the top of Mount Mayday during the typhoon. Every half an hour when the ship's bells sound, a geyser of water erupts into the air.

Typhoon Lagoon Basics

• Entry into Typhoon Lagoon is $69.03 for adults and $62.84 for children, including tax.
• Rental lockers are available throughout the park. The cost is $15 for a small locker and $20 for a large locker.
• Towels can be rented for $2.
• Lost children are taken to High 'N Dry Towels.

Reserved Seating and Cabanas

There are two areas that can be reserved at Typhoon Lagoon – both require wristbands to access which are given when checking in at the park:

• **Beachcomer Shacks** – There are 4 cabanas available to rent here, accommodating up to 6 guests each. The cost varies between $225 and $340, plus tax, depending on the season. Additional guests can be added for $25 each. Each cabana includes a one-day refillable drinks mug per person, a cooler with ice and bottled water, lounge furniture, rental towels, private lockers and waiter service. Reservations are made up to 180 days in advance at 407-WDW-PLAY. On the day reservations are subject to availability.

• **Getaway Glen** – This area includes 2 lounge chairs, an umbrella, a small table and two towels and is priced between $40 and $60, plus tax, for up to four people. Reservations can be made up to 180 days in advance by calling 407-WDW-PLAY. On the day reservations can be made at High N' Dry Towel Rental subject to availability. This is an option to guarantee a lounge chair, without turning up early.

Surfing School at Typhoon Lagoon

Typhoon Lagoon's wave pool is the perfect place to learn to surf. Several surf schools are provided by carefully selected schools. These run on selected dates very early in the morning.

Classes are of up to 13 people with 2 instructors, and are priced at $190 per person (including tax). Surfboards are provided.

Due to the early start time, regular hotel transportation is not available, but resort hotel buses run by the time the class ends. Book up to 90 days in advance by calling 407-WDW-PLAY.

Attractions

Mount Mayday

Humunga Kowabunga – Guests must be 48 inches (1.22m) or taller to ride. Reach speeds of up to 39mph and slide down five stories on each of the three enclosed "speed slides".

Gangplank Falls – A family slide with inner tubes connected for 4 people.

Storm Slides – Three body slides that twist and turn leaving riders in a splash pool at the bottom.

Mayday Falls – A tube slide that creates the feeling of being in "rough rapids".

Keelhaul Falls – A tube slide that spirals through a waterfall and cave.

Hideaway Bay

Crush n' Gusher – Guests must be 48 inches (1.22m) or taller to ride. A roller coaster-style water slide with one to three person rafts available – here you go both downhill and uphill with the help of high-pressure jets.

This is great fun and there are three different slides to choose from. Next to this attraction you will also find a beach area with lounge chairs and a small pool.

Miss Fortune Falls – Board this exciting family-raft attraction to spy the precious treasure artifacts collected by Captain Mary Oceaneer. This is the park's newest attraction and opened in Spring 2017.

Typhoon Lagoon

Home of the huge signature wave pool and sandy beaches to relax on.

Typhoon Lagoon Surf Pool – This star park attraction is the world's biggest outdoor wave pool. It alternates between 6-foot high surfing waves launched at 90 seconds intervals for 90 minutes, followed by small bobbing waves for 30 minutes.

Whatever setting the wave pool is on, waves are designed to be small by the time they reach the shore. A chalkboard at the edge of the beach posts the day's wave schedule. Inner tubes are not permitted in the lagoon.

Bay Slides – Several slides for toddlers. Guests must be 60 inches or shorter to ride.

Castaway Creek

A 2,100-foot lazy river that weaves through lush scenery around the whole park. Inner tubes are provided and a round trip takes 20 to 30 minutes.

Ketchakiddee Creek

A play area for younger kids with waterspouts and a small sandy beach. Guests must be 48 inches or shorter to ride the small slides in this area.

DINING:

Happy Landings Ice Cream - Snacks, No DDP, desserts are $4.50-$14
Leaning Palms - Snacks and Quick Service, DDP accepted, entrées are $7.50-$13
Let's Go Slurpin' - Bar, No DDP, drinks are $6-$13
Lowtide Lou's - Snacks and Quick Service, DDP, accepted entrées are $10-$11
Snack Shack - Snacks, No DDP, snacks are $9.50-$11.50
Typhoon Tilly's - Snacks and Quick Service, Snacks, DDP accepted, entrées are $9.50-$11

Disney Springs

The Disney Springs area is an exciting metropolis of restaurants, theaters and shops.

Disney Springs borders the south shore of Village Lake in the east-central portion of the Walt Disney World Resort.

The story of Disney Springs reflects that of many waterfront towns in Florida, where a natural spring was found by settlers who developed a village around it. Over time the small settlement grew into a full sized town.

Self-parking at Disney Springs is free. Valet parking is priced at $20.

Disney runs buses to and from Disney Springs from all on-site Disney resort hotels. Additionally, there are buses from the theme parks to Disney Springs from 4:00pm - but not from Disney Springs to the theme parks to avoid guests parking here for free and heading to the theme parks. To go from Disney Springs to a theme park you must go via a hotel.

There is boat transportation across Disney Springs if you do not wish to walk.

Bars and restaurants have varied opening and closing times but they are usually open between 10:30am and 11:30pm (with some locations opening as early as 8:30am for breakfast). Shops are generally open from 10:00am to 11:00pm Monday through Friday, and 10:00am to 11:30pm on weekends. Some locations are open later.

Entertainment

Amphicars – At The Boathouse, you can enjoy a guided tour on an amphicar that drives both on land and water. Pricing is $125 for up to 3 people with your own personal captain. Available from 10:00am to 10:00pm daily, weather permitting. A $25 discount is available with boutique or restaurant purchases of at least $50.
Bibbidi Bobbidi Boutique – A magical salon to transform your children into little princesses and princes. Prices range from $20 to $450, plus tax. For ages 3 and up.
Disney's Photopass Studio – Add professional-style individual or family photo-shoots to your PhotoPass account at no extra cost.
Marketplace Carousel – A small carousel.
Paradiso 37 Entertainment – Live entertainment in the evenings.
Raglan Road Live Music – Live Irish-inspired music outside the venue.

Disney Springs

AMC Movies
24 movie screens, with stadium-style seating in 18 theaters for unobstructed viewing. Includes six 'Fork & Screen' dine-in theaters.

House of Blues
Live music every night including blues, jazz, country and rock. Also home to the famous Gospel Brunch on Sundays.

Splitsville Luxury Lanes
A vintage, retro-style bowling alley with a fresh spin on music, dining and entertainment.

Aerophile - Balloon Flight
An iconic tethered balloon that sends guests soaring 400 feet into the sky, offering breath-taking views of the Walt Disney World Resort.

The VOID: Step Beyond Reality
By combining state-of-the-art virtual-reality technology, physical stages and multi-sensory effects—including touch and smell—The VOID invites you to become active participants in uniquely themed environments.

Surrounded by 3D imagery and sound in an immersive story by ILMxLAB and The VOID, you'll walk around freely without a tether as you explore an exciting new world.

At the time of writing both Star Wars and Wreck-It Ralph experiences are on offer. Pricing is from $30 per person for the experience. Guests must be 48" (122 cm) or taller and at least 10 years old to visit The VOID.

NBA Experience (Opening Summer 2019)
The state-of-the-art space will include interactive games and competitions, immersive experiences, a retail store and an adjacent restaurant.

No more information has been revealed at the time of writing.

Dining - Drinks Lounges

Dockside Margaritas – Drinks, No DDP, alcoholic drinks are $8-$19

Jock Lindsey's Hangar Bar – Bar with Snacks, No DDP, appetizers are $9-$16. Themed to Indiana Jones, with a prime location along Lake Buena Vista, the venue features unique cocktails and small plates.

Rainforest Café Lava Lounge – Bar and Quick Service, DDP accepted, appetizers are $11-$13, cocktails start at $11.

Stargazers Bar – Bar with Snacks, No DDP, appetizers are $7-$11, drinks are $7-$110.

Wine Bar George – Bar with Table Service food, No DDP, entrées are $13-$65, drinks are $9-$60.

Dining - Quick Service

Blaze Fast-Fire'd Pizza – Delicious pizzas ready in 180 seconds, DDP accepted, pizzas are $8-$10.

Bongo's Cuban Cafe Express – Cuban-inspired fast food, DDP accepted, sandwiches and wraps are $10-$12

Cookes of Dublin – Irish food, DDP accepted, entrées are $8-$13 at lunch and dinner.

D-Luxe Burger – American food, DDP accepted, burgers are $10-$13.

Earl of Sandwich – DDP accepted, sandwiches, salads and wraps are priced at $6-$8 each.

Food Truck Park – A permanent location for Disney Food Trucks selling food inspired by the parks. DDP accepted. Portions are $8.50 to $12 each.

Morimoto Asia Street Food - Pan-Asian cuisine, DDP accepted, entrées are $8-$10.

Pizza Ponte - Delicious pizzas, DDP accepted, pizzas are $7 by the slice or $9 for a sandwich.

The Polite Pig - Modern American BBQ flavors, DDP accepted, entrées are $11-$23.

The Smokehouse at House of Blues – American food, DDP accepted, entrées are $7-$14.

Wolfgang Puck Express – DDP accepted, entrées are $11-$18 at lunch and dinner. Breakfast options also available at $8-$13.

Dining - Table Service

AMC Disney Springs 24 Dine-In Theatres – American food, No DDP, entrées are $10-$17.

The Boathouse – American style, DDP accepted (2 credits), entrées are $17-$45. This restaurant features an upscale, waterfront dining experience with floating artwork and boats from the 30's, 40's & 50's. Its offerings include 3 bars, built over the water. Features steaks, chops, fresh seafood and a raw bar.

Bongos Cuban Café – Cuban food, DDP accepted, entrées are $22-$45.

Chef Art Smith's Homecomin' – This restaurant features Southern favorites. The "rustic-chic" restaurant has a glass-walled show kitchen and the Southern Shine Bar. DDP accepted. At lunch and dinner entrées are $16 to $30. At brunch entrées are $18-$26.

City Works Eatery & Pour House (opens Summer 2019) – The restaurant and bar will offer plenty of high-def TVs including a 165-inch screen, perfect for viewing your favorite live sporting events, and over 80 beers on tap.

The Edison – Themed to a 1920s-period power plant, recalling an exuberant era of invention and imagination. It features classic American food, craft cocktails and live entertainment, such as cabaret and music. DDP accepted. Entrées are $16-$22 at lunch and $24-$34 at dinner. On Thur, Fri and Sat evenings, there is a $10 cover charge from 10:00 p.m. Guests must be at least 21 years of age to enter The Edison after 10:00 p.m.

Enzo's Hideway – Italian-style eatery. DDP accepted, entrées are $15-$24. On Sunday evenings, a family-style feast is priced at $45 per adult and $19 per child.

Disney Springs

Frontera Cocina – American and Mexican food, DDP accepted, entrées are $14-$45.

House of Blues – American food, DDP accepted, entrées are $14-$30.

Jaleo by Jose Andres (Opens Late 2018) – Spanish cuisine, "an extensive menu of tapas that reflect the rich regional diversity of traditional and contemporary Spanish cuisine".

Maria & Enzo's – Italian cuisine, DDP accepted, entrées are $20-$28 at brunch, $13-$39 at lunch and $21-$44 at dinner.

Morimoto Asia – Pan-Asian cuisine, Signature Dining, DDP accepted (2 credits), entrées are $11-$45. There is a lighter 'late night' menu with entrées from $12-$17.

Paddlefish – Seafood, DDP accepted, entrées are $12-$70.

Paradiso 37, Taste of Americas – A variety of flavors, DDP accepted, entrées are $16-$34.

Planet Hollywood Observatory – American food, DDP accepted, entrées are $16-$30.

Rainforest Café – American food, DDP accepted, entrées are $16-$35.

Raglan Road Irish Pub and Restaurant – Irish food, DDP accepted, entrées are $16-$24 at lunch, $19-$30 at dinner, $13-$12 at brunch.

Splitsville Luxury Lanes – American food, DDP accepted, entrées are $11-$24.

STK Orlando – Rooftop Steakhouse, No DDP. Entrées are $39-$66 at lunch and $24-$67 at dinner, and $14-$54 at brunch.

T-REX – American food, DDP accepted, entrées are $17-$35.

Terralina Crafted Italian – No DDP, entrées are $14-$44.

Wolfgang Puck Bar & Grill (Opens Late 2018) – Mediterranean influenced dishes.

Dining - Specialty Food & Beverage and Snacks

Amorette's Patisserie – No DDP, pastries, cakes and crepes are $7 to $75.

AristoCrêpes – DDP accepted, crepes are $7-$9

B.B. Wolf's Sausage Co. – DDP accepted, sausage snacks are $6-$10.50

The Daily Poutine – Canadian food, poutine is $9.

Disney's Candy Cauldron – Sweets, candy and chocolates.

Erin McKenna's Bakery NYC – DDP accepted (snack credits), snacks are $2-$6.

The Ganachery – A chocolate lover's dream.

Ghirardelli Soda Fountain – No DDP, desserts are $6-$12, drinks are $2.50-$9.

Goofy's Candy Company – An assortment of candy, cookies, chocolates, frozen drinks and more.

Haagen Dazs – No DDP, ice cream and frozen beverages.

Sprinkles – Cupcakes, No DDP, cupcakes are $5, cookies are $3.50, ice creams are $5-$8 and shakes are $9-$10. The unique Cupcake ATM satisfies sweet-toothed epicureans 24/7.

Starbucks Marketplace – DDP accepted, drinks $3-$5. there is another location at the West Side of Disney Springs.

Vivoli il Gelato – No DDP, gelatos are $5 and milkshakes $10. Serves Panini sandwiches, espresso drinks and expertly crafted gelato made with fresh, seasonal ingredients.

Wetzel's Pretzels – No DDP, pretzels are $5.50-$7.

YeSake – No DDP, wraps and rolls are $9-$10.

Shops - Fashion and Sportswear

American Threads – Women's clothing inspired by the free American spirit.

Anthropologie – Women's apparel and accessories, shoes, beauty, home furnishings, gifts and decorative items.

Columbia – Apparel, footwear, accessories and equipment for outdoor and fishing.

Curl by Sammy Duvall – A high-end surf shop selling skateboards, surf wear and accessories.

DisneyStyle – Customized T-shirts in many colors, styles and themes.

Everything But Water – Designer swimwear, resortwear and accessories.

Fit2Run – Footwear. Use technology to find your perfect running shoe at this store. Then, test your shoe on the indoor running track.

francesca's – Unique, fashion-forward clothing, accessories, shoes, jewelry and gifts.

Free People – Casual women's apparel, shoes, accessories, activewear and gifts.

JOHNNY WAS – A curated selection of jewelry, books, and gifts and a signature line of colorful printed silk scarves, dresses, and tunics.

kate spade new york – From handbags and clothing to jewelry and fashion accessories.

LACOSTE – A unique and original lifestyle brand for all ages and genders.

Levi's – World famous Levi's Jeans and other apparel.

Lilly Pulitzer – Clothing and accessories in happy prints.

Lucky Brand – Vintage-inspired jeans and casual clothing with a rock and roll attitude.

Pele Soccer – Official team jerseys and soccer balls from dozens of teams.

Shore – Swimwear, fitness wear, everyday comfort clothing and exclusive products.

Stance – Stricking socks and boxer briefs.

Superdry – Clothing designs that fuse vintage Americana and Japanese-led graphics with British style.

Tommy Bahama – Island-inspired sportswear, denim, and swimwear for men and women.

Tren-D – Apparel and novel accessories for fashionable women.

Under Armour – Athletic apparel, footwear, and equipment for men, women, and youth.

UNIQLO – Casual apparel.

Volcom – Quality apparel, outerwear, footwear and accessories.

ZARA – Men's, women's and children's clothing and accessories.

Shops - Toys and Games

Dino-Store – Toys and 'Build-A-Dino'.

The LEGO Store – A dynamic retail store for famous LEGO bricks and toys with an interactive playground and towering LEGO displays indoors and out.

Once Upon A Toy – This 16,000 ft² toy store features fun new toys, games and collectibles.

Star Wars Galactic Outpost – Everything Star Wars in one place.

Shops - Jewelry and Accessories

ALEX AND ANI – Eco-conscious jewelry and accessories.

Chapel Hats – Just about every kind of headwear you can possibly imagine, including floppy hats, fedoras, sun hats, fascinators, outdoor hats, kids' styles and more!

Coach – Designer bags, apparel, outerwear, shoes and accessories.

Edward Beiner – Designer, fashion and performance eyewear.

Erwin Pearl – Offers a fine selection of enamel, precious and semi-precious fashion jewelry marked by style, creativity and outstanding quality.

Kipling – Lightweight and ultra-functional handbags, backpacks and luggage.

Luxury of Time by Diamonds International – Prominent designer watch brands and a large collection of fine jewelry.

Na Hoku: Hawaii's Finest Jewelers Since 1924 – Fine jewelry that captures the essence of Hawaiian Lifestyle.

Oakley – Eyewear, apparel and accessories.

PANDORA – Charm bracelets, necklaces, rings and earrings, as well as exclusive Disney-themed jewelry.

Something Silver – Classic and on-trend jewelry for every style.

Sunglass Icon – Sells a collection of designer sunglasses and eyewear.

TUMI – Premium travel, business and lifestyle accessories.

UNOde50 – Unique, highly hand-crafted jewelry designs.

Vera Bradley – A range of distinctive signature collections and specially-created Disney-themed products.

Shops - Footwear

Havaianas – Embody the fun, vibrant and spontaneous way of Brazilian life by fashioning your very own set of sandals. Or, take your pick from over 300 unique styles and colorful designs.

Johnston & Murphy – High-quality, well-crafted footwear and apparel.

Melissa Shoes – Stylish plastic footwear.

Sanuk – Put your best foot forward with creative designs crafted from yoga mats and other non-traditional materials.

Sperry – Sea-tested lifestyle products.

TROPHY ROOM – A unique athletic retail experience, inspired by the trophy room in the Jordan family estate.

UGG – A premium lifestyle brand offering footwear, loungewear, outerwear, and more.

Shops - Home, Decor, Gifts and Speciality

The Art of Disney – Disney animation art and collectibles from original paintings and prints to figurines and Vinylmation.

The Boathouse BOATIQUE – Nautical themed items.

Bongos Cuban Café Souvenir and Gift Shop – Latin themed merchandise.

Coca-Cola Store – Sells Coca-Cola merchandise and has a Coca-Cola Polar Bear experience and rooftop bar.

Crystal Art by Arribas Brothers – Glassware, crystal and metal artisan products; glassblowing; custom decorating.

Disney's Days of Christmas – Christmas collectibles, ornaments and Disney character holiday items.

Disney's Pin Traders – The premier location for pin trading at the Walt Disney World Resort.

Disney's Wonderful World of Memories – Disney scrapbook supplies, stationery and postcards.

House of Blues Gear Shop – House of Blues branded merchandise.

Marketplace Co-Op – This location houses several stores under one roof for Disney to test new retail concepts and boutiques before deciding whether to roll them out into fully fledged stores.

Mickey's Pantry – Make your abode magical with Disney home and kitchen products.

Orlando Harley-Davidson – Harley Davidson branded merchandise. There is also a photo opportunity inside.

Pop Gallery – Original, artist-signed sculptures and paintings, as well as upscale gift items.

Rainforest Café Retail Village – Rainforest Café themed merchandise.

Shop for Ireland – Irish themed merchandise and clothing. Located inside Ragland Road.

Sosa Family Cigars – Cigar store.

The Store at Planet Hollywood - Movie branded merchandise.

Sugarboo & Co. – Artful prints, home goods, paper products, accessories and more.

World of Disney Store – Centerpiece of Disney Springs, this 51,000 ft^2 retail palace is the biggest Disney shopping destination at the Walt Disney World Resort.

Shops - Beauty and Health

The Art of Shaving – Features high-end grooming essentials for the modern man: brushes, creams, razors, travel kits and more. You can even get a haircut and shave.

Basin – All-natural bath and skin care products.

Kiehl's since 1851 – Dermatologist recommended skin care solutions, hair care, body care, beauty & cosmetics.

M·A·C Cosmetics – A leader in professional makeup.

L'Occitane en Provence – International skincare and beauty company.

Origins – An organic skincare retailer with products made with natural oils.

Savannah Bee Company – Gifts and products made from locally grown, natural honey.

Sephora – Classic and up-and-coming cosmetic and fragrance brands.

Guests with Disabilities

This section covers procedures and accommodations Disney makes for guests visiting with disabilities. It covers people with mobility, hearing and visual impairments; facilities available at the resort hotels; and the Disability Access Card system for the theme parks.

Mobility

The Walt Disney World Resort strives to allow all Guests to utilize the main attraction entrances whenever possible, allowing the ride queuing system to be as fair as possible for all guests whatever their physical or mental abilities.

However, accessibility does vary from attraction to attraction within the Disney Parks – disabled guests should ask a Cast Member at the entrance to an attraction for the appropriate entrance. Sometimes guests can ride in their ECVs, other times they must transfer to a wheelchair, and other times they must transfer to a ride vehicle.

To rent a wheelchair, or ECV/motorized scooter for the day, proceed to the stroller shops located near the main entrance of each of the four theme parks, the Disney Springs Marketplace or the water parks. Guests may also bring their own into the parks.

If someone in your group with a disability needs to remain in a stroller while in the attraction queues, visit the Guest Relations lobby location near the entrance of any of the four theme parks to receive a "stroller as wheelchair" tag to be placed on the stroller.

Wheelchairs and ECVs rented at theme parks and the Disney Springs area are only for that specific location and must be returned before exiting. Length-of-stay rental tickets are available for a one-time payment, but wheelchairs or ECVs must still be returned before exiting each location.

Pricing is $12 per day for a wheelchair rental in the theme parks (you can use one receipt for rentals across multiple theme parks on the same day). Multi-day rentals are also available at $10 per day. ECV rentals are priced at $50 per day, plus a $20 refundable deposit in the theme parks. Outside vendors such as 'Buena Vista Scooters' rent ECVs at more affordable daily rates, usually from $30 to $40 per day.

All Walt Disney World resort transportation accommodates both wheelchairs and ECVs.

Hearing

Guests with hearing disabilities have the following accommodations for them at the theme parks: Assistive Listening systems, Reflective Captioning, Sign Language interpretation, Text Typewriter telephones, Handheld Captioning, Video Captioning and written aids.

Not every system is available at every location so be sure to ask Cast Members for help explaining what is available to aid you.

Some attractions are equipped with reflective captioning – simply inform the attractions Cast Members when entering the theater or attraction, and they will activate this feature.

> **WHAT ABOUT SPECIFIC INFORMATION?**
> If you require specific information regarding exact details of each attraction we strongly recommend you the Walt Disney World Resort's useful cognitive guide located at www.bit.ly/disndis.

Visual

Guests with visual disabilities have the following accommodations for them at the theme parks: Audio Description devices, Braille guidebooks and digital audio tours.

At the resort hotels

Examples of accommodations that are offered in resort hotels include wheelchair-accessible bathrooms, ramps and elevators, rooms designed for hearing impaired guests, and rooms that accommodate service animals. Accessible rooms can be booked online by using the "Accessible room" filter on the Walt Disney World Resort website, or by calling 407-939-7675 to discuss requirements in more detail.

Disability Access Service (DAS)

The Disability Access Service (DAS) is designed for guests with disabilities (including non-apparent disabilities) that are not able to wait in a normal queue line – their privileges will also extend to their party.

The DAS system can be activated from Guest Relations at each theme park – no proof of disability is required, but the Cast Member will ask you several screening questions in order to determine eligibility.

At Guest Relations, the disabled guest will have their photo taken, asked how many guests are in their party (limited to 6 maximum). This information is linked to all MagicBands/tickets in the party. The DAS system will be activated for 14 consecutive days. After 14 consecutive days, a guest will need to revisit Guest Relations to re-activate the system.

How does the system works?
A disabled guest goes to an attraction (or another party member on behalf of the DAS guest) and asks the Cast Member there to use the DAS system – the ride attendant will issue the guest with a return time (this will be the current wait time, minus 10 minutes). E.g. it is 2:00pm and the wait time for an attraction is 45 minutes – the guest will be issued with a 2:35pm return time. The return time is generated automatically by the system and cannot be changed by the Cast Member.

Until the return time, this guest can do whatever they wish. They can ride the attraction at any time after the return time. So, a guest could use their 2:35pm return time slot at 5:00pm, or they could return to ride at exactly 2:35pm. There is no early entry grace period for DAS system reservations.

Guests can view their return time on the My Disney Experience app or using in-park FastPass+ kiosks. This return time cannot be edited by guests or Cast Members.

Only one return time may be active at once – as soon as it has been used, another return time can be made for another attraction.

Alternatively, guests can cancel a return time, and reserve another attraction. The system can be combined with Fastpass+ and guests will still get the full FP+ entitlements, in addition to being able to use the system.

When it is time to ride, the DAS-eligible guest must be present at the ride entrance along with their party. They scan their MagicBand or park ticket and the whole of the party will be allowed entry. The reader will turn blue and the Cast Member will confirm that the DAS eligible guest is present and will be riding. If the DAS eligible guest does not wish to ride, the rest of the party must use the normal standby entrance.

There is a separate program for children with life-threatening illnesses, and wish-granting organizations. Disney says any guest who feels this system will not work for them should visit Guest Relations to work out a solution.

Activities outside the Parks

The Walt Disney World Resort offers much more than just theme parks and water parks. This chapter delves into this world of other possibilities.

ESPN Wide World of Sports

This 200-acre sports complex hosts both professional and amateur sports games. Facilities include three baseball fields, six NBA-sized basketball courts, softball courts, tennis courts, a track and field center, and beach volleyball courts.

Access to most amateur events can be purchased at the Box Office on-site. Adult tickets are priced at $18.50 and children's tickets are priced at $13.50. Park tickets with the 'Park Hopper Plus' option may be used for entry to some events.

Access to the venue is available via limited buses from the Disney's All-Star Resorts, Disney's Caribbean Beach Resort and Disney's Pop Century Resort. Free parking is also available.

Information on tickets is available on 407-939-GAME or at www.disneyworldsports.com.

Miniature Golf

The mini golf courses at the Walt Disney World Resort are surprisingly well priced - $14 for adults and $12 per child per round.

Disney's Fantasia Miniature Golf
This mini golf location consists of two different courses – Fantasia Gardens and Fantasia Fairways, both themed to the animated classic Fantasia.

Fantasia Gardens is perfect for those who are new to mini golf and kids; expect water effects, creative obstacles and great theming.

Fantasia Fairways is for the more experienced mini-golfers and can be more frustrating for younger children.

Fantasia Mini-golf is open daily from 10:00am to 11:00pm.

These courses are located on Epcot Resort Boulevard behind the Walt Disney World Swan Hotel and can be reached by taking a bus to either the Boardwalk or Swan hotels and walking from there – ask for directions at the concierge desks at either resort.

Disney's Winter Summerland Miniature Golf
This mini golf location features two different courses – a winter-themed course and a summer-themed course.

At the winter course your job is to make your way through the course towards the 'North Hole', while at the summer course you are surrounded by beach theming.

The two courses are located next to Blizzard Beach water park. You can drive there or take one of the resort buses. From Blizzard Beach it is less than a 5-minute walk to Winter Summerland mini golf.

Golf

The Walt Disney World Resort is home to four world-class golf courses that have won several awards – three of these are 18-holes and there is also a more leisurely 9-hole course.

The courses are:
- **Magnolia Golf Course** – The main hazard on this 18-hole course is water. Golf Digest rated this course 4 stars.
- **Lake Buena Vista Golf Course** – This 18-hole golf course has hosted the PGA Tour, the LPGA Tour and USGA events. Golf Digest rated this course 4 stars.
- **Palm Golf Course** – An 18-hole golf course.
- **Oak Trail Golf Course** – This 9-hole family friendly golf course is a walking distance course with a par of 36. There are even junior tees for the smaller family members. Pull carts can be rented.

Pricing:
- Pricing varies from $35 to $75 per person for each of the three 18-hole courses. The price for the Oak Trail Golf Course is $19 per junior (under 18) and $35 for adults. Disney hotel guests pay the lowest prices.
- Sunrise and Sunset rates are also often available at $35 for the 9-hole courses.
- 2-round and 3-round discounted passes are also available for purchase.
- Free transportation to all courses is available for Disney hotel guests.
- Professional club rentals are available for a fee - $40-$65 for Magnolia, Buena Vista and Palm – and $15 for Oak Trail (a partial set). Junior club rentals are free of charge at Oak Trail.
- 45-minute-long personal golf lessons are available. The pricing is $75 for adults and $50 for juniors aged 17 and under.
- Replay rates are available with a 50% discount off the full rate. Replays must be on the same day and cannot be reserved in advance.

Other information:
- The use of a golf cart is included in your greens fee for the courses. Carts are designed to be shared by two guests. To provide an enjoyable pace of play, players must use golf carts on the 3 championship courses.
- Proper golf attire is required at all the golf courses; denim jeans or casual shorts are not permitted.
- Reservations at Disney's Magnolia Golf Course are recommended but not necessary. Walk-up golfers will try to be accommodated.
- Disney recommends you arrive at least 30 minutes prior to your tee time to allow for check-in, cart assignment and a warm-up.
- For more detailed information on golfing, and to book tee times contact Disney directly on 407-WDW-GOLF or visit www.golfwdw.com.

Free activities outside the parks

Walt Disney World is no doubt an expensive place to visit - once you have factored in the price of getting there, staying in a hotel, park tickets, food and merchandise it is, more than likely, a trip that costs thousands of dollars.

Once you have paid for the basics, there are many more experiences that Disney offers to enhance your visit - whether it is dinner in Cinderella Castle with princesses, championship golfing or spa treatments; all these experiences come at a premium price.

However, there is no need to feel pressured into paying for extra experiences - there are many free things you can do to enhance your trip at no cost.

All the items in the list are accessible to everyone - there is no cost at all and they are all located outside the theme parks so you do not need tickets to take advantage of these activities.

1. Visit the resort hotels
This is one idea that many ignore, asking: "Why would you want to visit a hotel and not stay there?" and "How will that enhance my vacation?" It will. If you love the theming in the parks, then you absolutely must visit the different resort hotels.

From the relaxing beach at the Polynesian Village Resort, to the forest-feel of the Wilderness Lodge to the romanticism of Port Orleans, there is something for everyone.

Plus, you can combine your trip to a resort with a meal there. You do not need to be staying at the resorts to visit them and we cannot recommend this enough.

It really is possible to spend three or four days simply visiting and exploring the dozens of on-site Disney resort hotels. A must-do!

2. Movies under the stars
Almost all the Disney resort hotels offer nightly screenings of a Disney movie under the stars on a big screen. Chill out in one of the sun loungers sipping a cocktail while watching Toy Story or Fantasia.

3. Visit Disney's Boardwalk
This is a fun seaside-themed resort boardwalk area. Although there is not a huge amount to do here that is free, you can often enjoy live entertainment such as jugglers.

Or, you can explore the Boardwalk resort and grab a bite to eat in one of the many eating establishments.

Think of it as a miniature Disney Springs area with even more charm.

4. Enjoy the transportation
There are many ways to get between resorts and theme parks that are more relaxing than buses.

The monorail is a great way to get a birds-eye view of Magic Kingdom Park and Epcot. The ferryboat from the Transportation and Ticket Center to Magic Kingdom also offers great views.

The hidden gems, however, are the boats, which run between certain resorts and theme parks. The boat ride between Epcot and Hollywood Studios lasts about 25 minutes and you sail past some exquisite resort hotels.

If you want real luxury that makes you forget that you are at the world's most visited tourist destination, take the boat launches from the Wilderness Lodge to Fort Wilderness. This is a great, quaint, relaxing trip where all you see around you are trees and the lake.

Activities outside the Parks

Then, take the boat to the Contemporary resort and finally journey to Magic Kingdom Park.

The boats from Port Orleans, Old Key West and Saratoga Springs resorts to Disney Springs also offer beautifully relaxing moments.

5. Sing around a camp-fire
This is an example of free entertainment at the Walt Disney World Resort.

Every evening of the year you are able to join Chip n' Dale in a sing-along session around a camp-fire at the Fort Wilderness Resort. There are optional marshmallows available for purchase to roast on the fire.

The event usually runs at 8:00pm most of the year, but you can check the current timetable on the official Walt Disney World website.

This is the only way to get a free character meet and greet outside the theme parks! Plus, after the camp-fire, there is a movie shown under the stars.

6. Watch a free parade
Every evening the nighttime Electrical Water Pageant parade makes its way around the Seven Seas Lagoon in front of Magic Kingdom Park.

There are no characters involved and it is a very simple flotilla, but it is worth seeing at least once.

Plus, you can see the parade as you relax on the beach of any of the resort hotels around the lake!

AllEars.net provides the following information on the timetabling of this bit of free entertainment:
• Polynesian Village Resort: 9:00pm
• Grand Floridian: 9:15pm
• Wilderness Lodge: 9:35pm
• Fort Wilderness: 9:45pm
• Contemporary Resort: 10:05pm
• Magic Kingdom Park: 10:20pm (only during extended park hours).

When the Magic Kingdom fireworks are scheduled for 9:00pm, the Electrical Water Pageant runs 7 to 20 minutes later. After this, you could stick around and enjoy the next tip on this list.

7. Fireworks from Polynesian Village Resort Beach
If you want one of the best views of the Magic Kingdom fireworks, follow this tip.

Nothing can match standing in front of Cinderella Castle and feeling the awe of seeing the nightly fireworks explode before your eyes but for a different (and we'd say equally stunning) view, you need to make your way to the beach at the Polynesian Village Resort. Unfortunately you won't be able to clearly see the projections from this distance.

They even play the show music out of speakers at the Polynesian Village Resort beach when the show begins.

We recommend you sit further back on the beach, as the speakers are located along the back walkway area and not on the beach itself. Sometimes you might even get lucky and be able to grab a sun-lounger.

Aim to arrive at least 45 minutes before the fireworks are due to begin as this is fast becoming a well-known 'secret'.

Top Tip: We think the New Year and Fourth of July fireworks are even better from the Polynesian Village Resort beach than Magic Kingdom Park itself as these limited-time fireworks are 360-degree experiences that can be fully appreciated from the resort hotels,

Activities outside the Parks

something that can not be done when inside the park.

8. Do a free Walt Disney World Resort hotel tour
The Walt Disney World Resort offers many tours of the parks from the 'Wild Africa Trek' to the 'Keys to the Kingdom Tour'. If you are interested in these, check out our chapter dedicated to guided tours. They can cost in excess of $200 per person.

However, Disney also runs free tours of the unique resort hotels - granted they are much shorter, but they are an enlightening way to learn about the craftsmanship that goes into creating these settings at no cost. You do not need to be staying at the resorts to take these tours.

The 20-minute Sanaa Cultural Tour explores the Sanaa restaurant in detail. It runs at 4:00pm daily - check in at the podium of the Sanaa restaurant. No reservations. There are no guarantees, but sometimes this tour ends with a tasty treat too! You can call (407) 938-3000 to confirm this tour's schedule.

The Wonders of the Wilderness Lodge Tour is a one-hour tour explaining the backstory and design of the Wilderness Lodge Resort. The tour runs Wednesdays through Saturdays at 9:00am - ask at the lobby concierge for the exact meeting location. No reservations. Call (407) 824-3200 to confirm this tour's schedule.

The Culinary Tour at Animal

Kingdom Lodge is a culinary tour of both the Boma and Jiko restaurants lasting about 30 minutes in length. What's more, you get to sample some of the delights from these dining locations at no cost. The tour runs daily at 4:15pm - no reservations are required. The tour starts from the Boma podium. You can call (407) 938-3000 to confirm this tour's schedule.

Chapter Nineteen | Meeting the Characters

Meeting the Characters

Many people argue that a Walt Disney World Resort vacation is not complete without meeting some of the characters in the parks. After all, these are the characters many parents, let alone children, have grown up with and meeting them in real life can be a real dream come true.

In total, about 60 different characters meet in the parks daily.

Some character meets 'random' appearances that are not published on the park schedule, others are 'scheduled' meet and greets where you queue and take a photo, others are elaborate indoor experiences, and others like 'Enchanted Tales with Belle' are more like interactive shows.

You can also meet characters at select dining experiences.

If you need help finding a character, ask a Cast Member. Or, simply call 407-WDW-INFO.

Here we list character appearances that happen regularly and usually on a daily basis.

Magic Kingdom Park

- **Aladdin and Princess Jasmine** – Near *Aladdin's Magic Carpets* in Adventureland.
- **Alice in Wonderland and the White Rabbit** – Near *Mad Tea Party* in Fantasyland
- **Ariel** – In *Ariel's Grotto* (to the right of *Under the Sea*) in Fantasyland.
- **Aurora** – Behind *Cinderella Castle* (near Bibbidi Bobbidi Boutique).
- **Belle** – For those who participate in the show, you will be able to take a photo with Belle at *Enchanted Tales with Belle* in Fantasyland.
- **Buzz Lightyear** – In Tomorrowland between *Buzz Lightyear's Space Ranger Spin* and the *Carousel of Progress*.
- **Chip and Dale** – In Town Square.
- **Cinderella** – All day in *Princess Fairytale Hall* in Fantasyland.
- **Daisy Duck** – At *Pete's Silly Sideshow* in Fantasyland.
- **Donald Duck** – At *Pete's Silly Sideshow* in Fantasyland.
- **Elena of Avalor** – All day in Princess Fairytale Hall in Fantasyland.
- **Gaston** – Outside *Gaston's Tavern* in Fantasyland.
- **Goofy** – At *Pete's Silly Sideshow* in Fantasyland.
- **Marie from the Aristocats** – Near the flagpole at the front of the park before you reach Main Street, U.S.A.
- **Mary Poppins** – Near the flagpole at the front of the park before you reach Main Street, U.S.A.
- **Merida** – In Fairytale Garden, to the right of the castle
- **Mickey Mouse** – *Town Square Theater*. Mickey speaks at this location.
- **Minnie Mouse** – At *Pete's Silly Sideshow* in Fantasyland.
- **Peter Pan and Wendy** – Near *Peter Pan's Flight*.
- **Pluto** – Near the flagpole at the front of the park before you reach Main Street, USA.
- **Rapunzel** – All day in *Princess Fairytale Hall* in Fantasyland.
- **Snow White** – The front porch of *Town Square Theater*.
- **Tiana** – At Princess Fairytale Hall.
- **Tinker Bell** (and her fairy friends) – At Town Square Theater.
- **Winnie the Pooh and Tigger** – In Fantasyland, to the left of the entrance by *The Many Adventures of Winnie the Pooh*.

Meeting the Characters

Epcot

- **Aladdin and Princess Jasmine** – Morocco Pavilion
- **Anna and Elsa** – Norway Pavilion
- **Alice** (in Wonderland) – UK Pavilion
- **Baymax** – Epcot Character Spot
- **Belle** – France Pavilion
- **Donald Duck** – Mexico Pavilion
- **Daisy Duck** – By *Spaceship Earth*.
- **Joy and Sadness** (from Inside Out) – Epcot Character Spot
- **Mary Poppins** – UK Pavilion
- **Mickey, Minnie and Goofy** – Epcot Character Spot
- **Mulan** – China Pavilion
- **Snow White** – Germany Pavilion

Top Tip: Between the Canada and UK pavilions there is a large gate. Sometimes there are unplanned meet and greets here before 3:00pm. This also happens at the gates to the left of the American Adventure pavilion, in a narrow outdoor area.

Disney's Animal Kingdom

- **Chip and Dale** – In Dinoland USA.
- **Donald** – In Dinoland USA.
- **Doug and Russell** (from Up) – Near the entrance to *It's tough to be a bug*.
- **Goofy** – In Dinoland USA.
- **Mickey and Minnie** (together) – At Adventurers Outpost.
- **Pocahontas** – *Discovery Island Character Landing*, opposite Flame Tree Barbecue
- **Pluto** – In Dinoland USA.
- **Rafiki** – At *Rafiki's Planet Watch*.
- **Scrooge McDuck** – In Dinoland USA.

Disney's Hollywood Studios

- **Buzz Lightyear, Woody and Green Army Men** – Near *Toy Story Midway Mania*
- **Chip & Dale** – In front of the Chinese Theater.
- **Doc McStuffins** – In Animation Courtyard, just outside *Disney Junior*.
- **Donald and Daisy** – In front of the Chinese Theater.
- **Goofy** – In front of the Chinese Theater.
- **Jake** (of the Neverland Pirates) – In Animation Courtyard, outside *Disney Junior*.
- **Mickey** (in his Sorcerer costume) and **Minnie** – At Red Carpet Dreams, opposite Sci-Fi Diner.
- **Olaf** – At *Celebrity Spotlight*, by Echo Lake.
- **Pluto** – In front of the Chinese Theater.
- **Sofia the First** – In Animation Courtyard, just outside *Disney Junior*.
- **Star Wars Characters** – Inside *Star Wars Launch Bay*

Top Tip: If you want to meet rare characters with little to no wait, then you will be excited to hear about "Character Palooza!" – an unpublished meet and greet that takes place at Disney's Hollywood Studios. This event, which is hosted randomly from 3:00pm to 7:00pm, is an insider's secret and only takes place on days when Fantasmic is performing. The location changes constantly but it at one of three places: the Streets of America, around Echo Lake, or at the gates near Tower of Terror. From experience, it seems to take place more often at the last location.

> **CHARACTER TIPS:**
> - Character wait times can be as long as the wait times for popular rides.
> - Do not force children to interact with characters, especially if they are very young.
> - Chat to the face characters and get an insight into their lives.
> - There are more characters out in the mornings and early afternoons than during the evenings.
> - Characters may have limited vision so be aware of their blind spots. They may not be able see what is to their side or even directly in front of them.
> - Characters can sign anything; except what you are wearing.
> - Characters may not hold children or infants.
> - Do not be angry if the character needs to go away for a few minutes.
> - Some characters cannot talk – no matter how hard you try.
> - Be courteous and do not hurt the characters. They have feelings too!

Character Dining

If you want to combine eating with meeting the characters, then character-dining experiences are a great option for you. You don't even need to wait to meet the characters as they come round to every table.

In our opinion, the food is not usually the best at these types of places. Although the food is definitely not *bad*, but you are definitely paying more for the entertainment than for gourmet food.

• **Alice in Wonderland** – 1900 Park Fare, Grand Floridian (Breakfast only);
• **Aurora** – Princess Storybook Breakfast/Lunch/Dinner (Norway pavilion, Epcot)
• **Beast** – Be Our Guest Restaurant (dinner only, Magic Kingdom)
• **Chip n Dale** – Garden Grill (Breakfast, Lunch and Dinner, Epcot)
• **Cinderella** (and also sometimes Prince Charming) – 1900 Park Fare, Grand Floridian (Dinner only); Cinderella's Royal Table (Magic Kingdom); Akershus Royal Banquet Hall (Norway pavilion, Epcot)
• **Donald Duck** – Tusker House in Disney's Animal Kingdom (Other Ducks visit too at this location – Breakfast and Lunch); Cape May Café at Beach Club (Breakfast only); Chef Mickey's at Contemporary Resort (Brunch and Dinner)
• **Disney Junior Characters** (Sofia the First and Doc McStuffins) – Hollywood and Vine (Breakfast and Lunch, Disney's Hollywood Studios)
• **Lady Tremaine, Anastasia** and **Drizella** – 1900 Park Fare, Grand Floridian (Dinner only)
• **Lilo and Stitch** – Ohana's Best Friends Breakfast, Polynesian Village Resort.
• **Goofy** – Cape May Café at Beach Club (Breakfast only); Chef Mickey's at Contemporary Resort (Brunch and Dinner); Tusker House at Animal Kingdom
• **Mad Hatter** – 1900 Park Fare, Grand Floridian (Breakfast only);
• **Mary Poppins** – 1900 Park Fare, Grand Floridian (Breakfast only), Princess Storybook Breakfast/Lunch/Dinner (Norway pavilion, Epcot)
• **Mickey Mouse** – Garden Grill (Breakfast, Lunch and Dinner, Epcot); Chef Mickey's at Contemporary Resort (Brunch and Dinner); Mickey's Backyard BBQ (and other popular characters, Dinner only, Fort Wilderness Resort & Campground); Ohana's Best Friends Breakfast, Polynesian Village Resort;
• **Minnie Mouse** – Cape May Café, Beach Club (Breakfast only); Chef Mickey's at Contemporary Resort (Brunch and Dinner)
• **Pluto** – Garden Grill (Breakfast, Lunch and

Dinner, Epcot); Chef Mickey's at Contemporary Resort (Brunch and Dinner); Ohana's Best Friends Breakfast, Polynesian Village Resort.
• **The Princesses, including Cinderella** – Cinderella's Royal Table (Magic Kingdom); Akershus Royal Banquet Hall (Norway Pavilion, Epcot)
• **Winnie the Pooh, Tigger, Piglet** and **Eeyore** – Crystal Palace (Magic Kingdom), 1900 Park Fare, Grand Floridian (Breakfast only).

None of these character appearances are guaranteed but they are a good indication of which characters you can expect to see at each location.

One more thing:
Garden Grove at the Swan Hotel is another character buffet location, but we have never seen Mickey or Minnie here. You can usually expect to see Goofy and Pluto, or Rafiki and Timon. Characters only appear at select meals - check with the hotel before reserving.

Chapter Twenty | Doing Disney on a Budget

Doing Disney on a Budget

Although visiting the Walt Disney World Resort is not exactly cheap, it can be done on a budget, and you can still have a fantastic trip while saving some cash. Follow these tips and reap the savings!

Traveling to Walt Disney World

Driving – If you are located in the US, driving can be a good option and save you a lot of money compared to flying. Remember to factor in the price of tolls and fuel.

Budget flights – Starting at under $100, these can be great value if booked far in advance. Also watch out for last minute sales or use loyalty points!

Planning

1. Staying On-Site – Do you really need a Disney on-site hotel? They are convenient but they are often significantly more expensive than off-site hotels.

Remember to factor in other costs like resort fees, taxes, parking charges and transport costs when comparing prices.

2. Buy an annual pass – If you plan on visiting more than twice in the same year, buying an annual pass can be a great money saver. If staying off-site, you will not need to pay for parking with an annual pass.

It can also save you a lot of money on hotels, dining and merchandise.

3. Wait for a special offer – The Walt Disney World Resort often runs special offers – whether it is discounted room prices or free dining, so keep an eye out for these. Free dining offers, in particular, can save you a lot of money.

4. Downgrade your hotel – Do you really need a luxurious Disney hotel? Will you ever use the extra amenities you are paying for? If not, but you still want to stay on property, then downgrade to somewhere like the All-Star or Pop Century resorts.

5. Tickets – Pre-purchase tickets online at reputable websites such as undercovertourist.com – there are savings of up to $77 per person compared to buying from Disney.

In addition, UK visitors should consider purchasing the exclusive Ultimate Tickets in advance in the UK, instead of buying tickets at American prices.

6. Quieter times – By visiting when the parks are less busy, you will be able to do more each day meaning you can spend less days in the parks, which ultimately means a cheaper and more relaxing vacation. See our quiet times section of this guide.

Tickets during less busy (off-peak) times are also cheaper than during peak periods.

Doing Disney on a Budget

At the Parks

1. Do not purchase a dining plan – Although the dining plans claim savings of up to 40%, if you do not eat a lot, or eat the cheaper options at restaurants, it is cheaper to pay for each meal separately.

2. Packed lunches – You can make your own packed lunches, such as sandwiches, and take them into the parks. If you have a car, drive to a nearby supermarket for supplies.

3. Eat meals off-site – If you have a car, drive off-property and eat at restaurants outside of the Walt Disney World Resort. These are a fraction of the cost – remember, though, that it may take a while to get from the theme parks to an off-property restaurant.

4. Have Table Service meals at lunch – Table Service meals and buffets can be substantially cheaper at lunch than at dinner. Sometimes the food on offer is different; sometimes it is exactly the same.

5. Take your own photos – If you do not want to pay $15 or $20 for a character photo, simply take one yourself, ask another guest, or ask a Cast Member who will be happy to help.

6. Take your own costumes/plushes – If your little boy or girl will want to buy a dress or outfit in the parks, these are substantially cheaper online, at supermarkets or anywhere off Walt Disney World Resort property. Just buy them and pack them secretly. Give your child the costume once you arrive and they will be over the moon. The same applies to Disney plushes and toys.

7. More affordable meals – Although Disney food is expensive, there are some better value meals than others. Kids Quick Service meals, in particular, are great value and include a drink, whereas adult meals do not.

Remember that if you do not want fries or a side with a meal, they can be removed and save you money – everything can be ordered a la carte.

Or alternatively, have a late lunch buffet and then just have a smaller snack for dinner.

8. Use FastPass+ – It will save you hours of time in queue lines, meaning you can spend fewer days in the park, and save on food and park ticket costs.

Dining

There are a huge variety of places to eat at the Walt Disney World Resort, from sandwiches to fast food to table service dining, character buffets and even signature dining options.

Restaurant Types

Buffet restaurants – Fill up your plate from the food offered as many times as you want. A variation is "family style" meals where servers/waiters come around to tables and offer food.
Quick Service – Fast food. Everything from burgers and chips, to chicken to pizza and pasta, as well as more exotic options.
Table Service – Restaurants where you order from a menu, and are served by a waiter/server.
Character buffets – All-you-can eat locations where characters visit each table to interact for photos while you dine.
Signature Dining Experiences – The most exquisite dining experiences. These require two Table Service credits for guests on Disney Dining Plans.
Dinner Shows – A meal (usually buffet or family style) is included in the price, as well as your entertainment for the evening. Dinner shows cost two Table Service credits for guests on Dining Plans.

Disney Dining Plans

The Disney Dining Plans are pre-paid dining credits that allow you to eat at almost any dining location without worrying about the cost – because it has all been paid for in advance!

The plans are available to guests who book a vacation package with park tickets and a hotel, as well as Disney Vacation Club point bookings.

Guest are allotted a number of 'credits' for each night of their stay for Table Service meals, Quick Service meals and Snacks. The number of credits depends on the plan purchased. Credits are redeemed for meals.

You are given all your credits as a lump sum at the beginning of your vacation; you choose how and when to use these by midnight on the night you check out.

Disney claims you can save up to 40% by purchasing the dining plans but this relies on you always eating the most expensive items.

You must book the Disney Dining Plans for the whole duration of your stay. To get around this you can make two back-to-back hotel reservations, and only add a Dining Plan to one.

Top Tip: Make sure to present your MagicBand before ordering – restaurants often have two menus, with one specifically for those on the Disney Dining Plan.

> **TOP TIPS**
>
> 1: You do not have to order from the set menu, although it may save you money if you do. Ordering an item separately (a la carte) is completely fine.
>
> 2: Disney sometimes offers free dining to guests staying at its resort hotels that also book park tickets at the same time – if this offer is available, grab it with both hands as it can save you a significant amount of money.
>
> 3: Disney offers an allergy-friendly menu at almost all its Quick Service and Table Service restaurants. The allergy-friendly menus cover the most common allergies, including gluten/wheat, milk, peanut, nut and fish. If a guest still wishes to speak to a chef, that option is still available.

Gratuities are not included with the dining plans except for Dinner Shows, Private In-Room Dining and at Cinderella's Royal Table. An automatic 18% gratuity charge will be added to your bill for parties of 6 or more.

Merchandise or photo products that may be offered at some Character Dining Experiences are not included.

Here we list what is include per night of your stay with each dining plan for 2019.

Quick-Service Dining Plan
$52.50 per adult per night, $23.78 per child (ages 3-9).
• 2 Quick-Service meals (1 meal = entrée and non-alcoholic beverage)
• 2 Snacks
• 1 refillable resort mug per person per stay (worth $18.99, plus tax)

Dining Plan
$75.49 per adult per night, $27.98 per child.
• 1 Quick-Service meal
• 1 Table-Service meal (1 meal = entrée and non-alcoholic beverage at breakfast OR entrée, dessert and non-alcoholic beverage at lunch and dinner. At a buffet meal you will receive access to the full buffet and a beverage)
• 2 snacks
• 1 refillable resort mug per person per stay (worth $18.99, plus tax)

Deluxe Dining Plan $116.25 per adult per night, $43.49 per child.
• 3 Table-Service or Quick-Service meals. You can choose for maximum flexibility. With the deluxe plan you also get an appetizer at Table Service locations, in addition to an entrée, dessert and non-alcoholic beverage.
• 2 snacks
• 1 refillable resort mug per person per stay (worth $18.99, plus tax)

Guests can choose to substitute one Quick-Service meal for an apple, a bottle of soda and a bag of potato chips, or one Table-Service meal for 3 eligible snacks in one transaction. This is available at select locations.

We do not recommend doing this as you will be losing a lot of the value of your plan, and most people end up with unused snack credits anyway - if you are a fan of snacks, however, this may work well for you.

At the end of your meal when you ask for the check, you will receive a receipt stating how many credits you used for that meal and how many remain. If you have bought several Dining Plans together, this number will be the sum of all your party's credits. You are free to order off-menu items and pay for these separately.

Reservations are strongly recommended for all Table Service restaurants - check menus at Disney.go.com/dining in advance to decide.

Reservations and Cancellations

To eat at Table Service restaurants, we strongly recommend making a reservation. These can be made up to 180 days in advance at 407-WDW-DINE or online. At certain popular dining locations, such as Cinderella's Royal Table, you need to make reservations exactly 180 days in advance to avoid disappointment during busier times of the year.

A credit or debit card is required when making dining reservations. Cancellations should be made the day before by 11:59pm; if they are not, a $10 per person charge will apply for no-shows. For prepaid locations such as dinner shows, the full cost of the meal will be retained for no-shows. Cancellations can be made at 407-WDW-CNCL, on the MyDisneyExperience website, at Guest Services or at any restaurant.

Guests can also make last-minute dining reservations up to 20 minutes in advance using the My Disney Experience website and iOS mobile app.

Dress Codes

At all the theme park restaurants, the dress code is simply what you would wear in the theme parks – whether that is a shirt or a tank top, pants or shorts, shoes or flip flops.

The following Signature Restaurants (all located at resort hotels) have a resort casual/business casual dress code:
• Artist Point at Disney's Wilderness Lodge
• California Grill at the Contemporary Resort
• Cítricos at the Grand Floridian Resort & Spa
• Flying Fish Cafe at Disney's BoardWalk
• Jiko – The Cooking Place at Disney's Animal Kingdom Lodge
• Narcoossee's at Disney's Grand Floridian Resort & Spa
• Yachtsman Steakhouse at Disney's Yacht and Beach Club Resorts

Men's dress code: Dress slacks, jeans, trousers, or dress shorts, short- or long-sleeved shirt with a collar or t-shirt required. Jackets are optional.

Ladies dress code: Jeans, skirt, or dress shorts with blouse, sweater or t-shirt, or a dress required.

Not permitted: Tank tops, swimsuits or cover-ups, hats for men, cut offs, torn clothing, or t-shirts with offensive language or graphics.

Victoria and Albert has a much stricter dress code, which you should ask about when making your reservation.

CAST MEMBER INSIGHT

The author says: "I cannot stress the importance of making advanced restaurant reservations.

When I worked as a Cast Member in the parks, Guests would often ask me how they could eat at a certain restaurant that day.

I would advise that guests check with restaurants for no-show or cancellations, but that reservations were accepted up to 6 months in advance. The chance of guests finding a same-day Table Service meal, however, is extremely low.

On occasion, I would want to eat somewhere with friends without a reservation. We never managed to get a table on the same day as restaurants were always fully booked. Solution: Book well in advance. Alternatively, try the restaurants at the resort hotels that often have space for walk-ins - many of these are excellent and uncrowded."

Useful to Know

There are many elements that can make or break a Walt Disney World vacation. This chapter covers important things to consider such as when to visit, as well as park services such as Single Rider Queue Lines and Photopass options.

Photopass and Memory Maker

Throughout the theme parks you will find Photopass photographers ready to take your photo in front of the major park landmarks, at character meet and greets and at other experiences too.

Photopass:
Photopass is a service which works with a special card which you are given, at no cost, the first time you have a Photopass photo taken. You then use this same card every time you take photos, handing it to the photographer for them to scan. Once your vacation is over, enter the unique code printed on your Photopass card into the Photopass website and you can see all your photos. From there, you can have your photos added to souvenirs, order individual prints or pay for individual photo downloads.

Memory Maker:
Memory Maker is the name of a photo package which allows you to purchase all your Photopass photos at once. This includes in-park photos, character photos and attraction photos on one account.

Photos are available for download from the day they were taken until 45 days later. You have 30 days from the date of your first download to take more pictures with your Memory Maker account.

Memory Maker must be purchased at least 3 days before the beginning of your trip to get all your photos. It is available in advance for $169 or can be bought at Walt Disney World for $199. If you have a MagicBand, simply tap it each time to get your photos in the park. You can also buy a physical CD archive with all your pictures for an additional $30, or you can download the photos at no cost.

Digital dining photos from Chef Mickey's, Hoop-Dee-Doo Revue, Tusker House breakfast, 'Ohana breakfast, 1900 Park Fare and Spirit of Aloha dinner show are also included.

Guests who purchase Memory Maker in advance, link it to their My Disney Experience account and wear a MagicBand on rides have their attraction photos automatically added to their account without needing to stop at the ride photo counter. The ride photo at Frozen Ever After is exclusively available to MagicBand wearers.

In addition, riders with MagicBands on *The Twilight Zone: Tower of Terror* and *Seven Dwarfs Mine Train* have an on-ride video montage added automatically to their account.

Although on-ride photos are usually linked automatically, it is still worth adding them manually as there can be errors. To do this, when you get off a ride and see the photo screens, simply tap your MagicBand on the reader below your photo.

For guests visiting for a short period of time, a one-day Memory Maker package is available for purchase for $69. Guests will receive unlimited

Useful to Know

digital downloads for one day, including downloads for all photos captured by PhotoPass Photographers, at Meet and Greet locations and select attractions and dining locations. Guests can purchase the 'Memory Maker One Day' via the My Disney Experience app after having linked one photo.

Top Tip 1: Pre-purchase MemoryMaker in advance at https://disneyworld.Disney.go.com/memory-maker/ to save $30. This must be done at least 3 days before your first photo is taken.

Top Tip 2: Take a photo of your Photopass card and its barcode, that way if you lose the card you still have access to all the photos on it.

Top Tip 3: You can have multiple Photopass cards and add them all to one online account in one go.

On-ride Photos

Many of Disney's rides have specially placed cameras positioned to take perfectly framed photos of you on the ride. After the ride, you can purchase these photos and save the memory.

You do not have to buy on-ride photos straight after your ride; you can pick them up at any time during the day. Just remember your unique number at the attraction exit or ask a member of staff at the photo kiosk to write it down for you.

If you like the photo - buy it! These photos capture memories you will treasure.

Single Rider Queue Lines

One of the best ways to significantly reduce your time waiting in queue lines is to use the Single Rider line instead of the regular queue line. This is a completely separate queue line that is used to fill free spaces on ride vehicles - guests who join this queue will ride individually.

As an example of how the system works: if a ride vehicle can seat 8 people and a group of 4 turns up, followed by group of 3 in the regular line, then a guest from the Single Rider line will fill the empty space.

If the park does get extremely busy then Single Rider lines can be closed. This happens when the wait for Single Riders is the same or greater than the regular line, undermining its purpose. If the park is not very busy then sometimes these queue lines do not operate either.

Groups can use the Single Rider queue line; they will not ride with each other but can still meet after riding at the exit of the ride

The following rides have single rider queue lines:
• Expedition Everest (Animal Kingdom)
• Rock n Roller coaster (Hollywood Studios)
• Test Track (Epcot)

Extra Magic Hours

Each day Disney resort hotel guests are allowed 1-hour early entry into one theme park, and can stay up to 2 hours after regular park closing at another park.

During these extended opening hours, queue lines are typically much shorter than during the day time. Each member of your party needs a valid resort ID to access attractions during these extended hours.

The exact parks open during Extra Magic Hours (EMH) vary week to week and can be seen online up to 6 months in advance on the Walt Disney World website.

How can I get Extra Magic Hours?
They are available exclusively to guests staying at Walt Disney World resort hotels and select partner properties. Annual pass holders not staying at Disney hotels are not entitled to EMH.

What rides are available during EMH?
Unfortunately, not all rides are open during these extended hours, but most popular rides are open. The following is a list of attractions that typically participate in Extra Magic Hours.

Magic Kingdom Park:
Extra Magic Hours attractions are: Astro Orbiter, The Barnstormer, Big Thunder Mountain (evening only) Buzz Lightyear's Space Ranger Spin, Country Bear Jamboree (evening only), Dumbo the Flying Elephant, Haunted Mansion (evening only) "it's a small world", Mad Tea Party, The Magic Carpets of Aladdin (evening only), The Many Adventures of Winnie the Pooh, Mickey's PhilharMagic, Monsters, Inc. Laugh Floor (evening only), Peter Pan's Flight, Pirates of the Caribbean (evening only), Prince Charming Regal Carrousel, Seven Dwarfs Mine Train, Space Mountain, Swiss Family Treehouse (evening only, Tomorrowland Speedway, Tomorrowland Transit Authority PeopleMover (morning only), Under the Sea ~ Journey of the Little Mermaid and Walt Disney's Carousel of Progress (morning only).

Epcot:
Extra Magic Hours attractions are: Advanced Training Lab (evening only), The American Adventure (evening only), American Heritage Gallery (evening only), Disney & Pixar Short Film Festival (evening only), Epcot Character Spot (evening only), Frozen Ever After, Gran Fiesta Tour Starring The Three Caballeros (evening only), Journey Into Imagination With Figment (evening only), Living with the Land, Mission: SPACE (evening only), O Canada! (evening only), Project Tomorrow: Inventing the World of Tomorrow, The Seas with Nemo & Friends, Soarin' Around the World, Spaceship Earth, Test Track and Turtle Talk With Crush

(evening only).

Disney's Hollywood Studios:
Extra Magic Hours attractions are: Alien Swirling Saucers, Rock 'n' Roller Coaster Starring Aerosmith, Slinky Dog Dash Star Tours: The Adventures Continue, Toy Story Mania! and The Twilight Zone Tower of Terror.

Currently EMHs only operate in the morning at this park.

Disney's Animal Kingdom Park:
Extra Magic Hours attractions are: Avatar Flight of Passage, DINOSAUR, Expedition Everest, Gorilla Falls Exploration Trail (subject to availability). It's Tough to be a Bug!, Kilimanjaro Safaris (subject to availability), Na'vi River Journey, Primeval Whirl and TriceraTop Spin.

Currently EMHs only operate in the morning at this park.

When to Visit

Crowds at the Walt Disney World Resort vary greatly from season to season and even day to day. The difference of a single day can save you hundreds of dollars, as well as hours waiting in lines. You will have to consider school vacations and national holidays from the US and other nearby countries. Other factors that affect visitor numbers include the weather and pricing.

Here is our list of when we think are the best times to visit the Walt Disney World Resort. These are based on both crowd levels and room prices. These are our best estimates, but they are still estimates! Weeks are rated from 1 to 10, with 1 being the absolute best time of the year to visit (very low crowds and the cheapest prices) and 10 being the worst (very high crowds and the most expensive prices).

Week starting	Score	Week starting	Score	Week starting	Score
Dec 3, 2018	5	Apr 15, 2019	7	Aug 26, 2019	4
Dec 10, 2018	4	Apr 22, 2019	6	Sep 2, 2019	3
Dec 17, 2018	7	Apr 29, 2019	5	Sep 9, 2019	3
Dec 24, 2018	9	May 6, 2019	5	Sep 16, 2019	3
Dec 31, 2018	10	May 13, 2019	5	Sep 23, 2019	4
Jan 7, 2019	5	May 20, 2019	6	Sep 30, 2019	4
Jan 14, 2019	4	May 27, 2019	6	Oct 7, 2019	5
Jan 21, 2019	5	Jun 3, 2019	6	Oct 14, 2019	5
Jan 28, 2019	3	Jun 10, 2019	7	Oct 21, 2019	5
Feb 4, 2019	4	Jun 17, 2019	8	Oct 28, 2019	5
Feb 11, 2019	6	Jun 24, 2019	8	Nov 4, 2019	5
Feb 18, 2019	7	Jul 1, 2019	10	Nov 11, 2019	5
Feb 25, 2019	4	Jul 8, 2019	9	Nov 18, 2019	5
Mar 4, 2019	6	Jul 15, 2019	8	Nov 25, 2019	9
Mar 11, 2019	7	Jul 22, 2019	8	Dec 2, 2019	4
Mar 18, 2019	8	Jul 29, 2019	8	Dec 9, 2019	4
Mar 25, 2019	8	Aug 5, 2019	8	Dec 16, 2019	7
Apr 1, 2019	8	Aug 12, 2019	6	Dec 23, 2019	9
Apr 8, 2019	7	Aug 19, 2019	5	Dec 30, 2019	10

Note that Saturday and Sundays are usually much busier than on other days of the week, as are public holidays and the two or three days before and after these holidays. January and February are often months when major attractions go down for their annual refurbishment.

Rider Switch

Rider Switch is a system that enables a group to take turns riding an attraction while only needing to queue once. An example use is when a child is too small and adults take turns riding so the other can stay with the child.

To use Rider Switch, simply ask a Cast Member at an attraction entrance to use the service.

Group 1 (for example, the father) will go through the normal queue line and Group 2 (for example, the mother) will be given a Rider Switch Pass. Once the first adult has ridden, they simply hand the child to the second adult who presents the Rider Switch Pass at the entrance and they will be given expedited entry. Up to two people may ride with this pass.

Rider Switch is available at: The Barnstormer, Big Thunder Mountain Railroad, Seven Dwarfs Mine Train, Space Mountain, Splash Mountain, Stitch's Great Escape, Tomorrowland Indy Speedway, Frozen Ever After, Mission: SPACE, Soarin', Test Track, Disney's Hollywood Studios, Alien Swirling Saucers, Rock 'n' Roller Coaster Starring Aerosmith, Slinky Dog Dash, Star Tours - The Adventures Continue, Twilight Zone Tower of Terror, Avatar Flight of Passage, DINOSAUR, Expedition Everest, Kali

River Rapids and Primeval Whirl.

As of 2018, this system is currently moving from paper-based Rider Switch passes to a digital system using MyDisneyExperience and MagicBands and/or park cards.

Park Regulations

Park regulations are in place for the safety and comfort of all guests and Cast Members.

Here are some notable park regulations which you should be aware of:
• Proper attire, including shoes and shirts, must be worn at all times. Anyone wearing inappropriate attire may be removed from the park.
• Smoking of tobacco, e-cigarettes or other products that produce a vapor or smoke are allowed only in designated areas.
• Guests under age 14 must be accompanied by another guest age 14 or older to enter the theme parks, water parks and DisneyQuest. To board attractions, guests under 7 years old must be accompanied by someone age 14 or older.
• Recreational devices with wheels such as skateboards, scooters, skates or shoes with built in wheels are not permitted in the parks.
• Strollers larger than 36" (92cm) by 52" (132cm) are not permitted.
• Any item of baggage or a cooler larger than 24" (61cm) long x 15" wide (38cm) by 18" high (46cm) is not permitted in the parks.
• Any trailer-like item that is pushed or towed by a person or a machine is not permitted in the parks.
• Weapons, masks, folding chairs, large tripods, glass containers, alcoholic beverages, illegal substances, and animals which are not service animals are not permitted in the parks.
• Balloons, plastic straws and drink lids are not permitted at Disney's Animal Kingdom Park for the safety of the animals.
• Selfie sticks are banned from all Disney theme parks and water parks.

Useful to Know

Assorted Questions & Answers

What currency do I need?
US Dollars. If necessary, either exchange money before you go into cash or use a debit or credit card. Beware of charges from your bank. Travellers' checks are not widely accepted.

For international visitors, we would recommend using a pre-paid debit card such as FairFx (UK readers can waive the £9.95 card fee through our exclusive link - http://bit.ly/debitdlp) where you load local currency on and it is converted into dollars. This way there are no exchange fees when making transactions in the USA.

Is there a time difference?
Florida is part of the Eastern Standard Time zone. That means it is -5 hours from UTC. So 5:00pm in London is midday in Florida (except during a few weeks when the clocks change in the US before the UK).

Due to there being so many time zones in the US, and around the world, it is impossible to cover them all here. Eastern Standard Time Zone is 3 hours ahead of Pacific time – so midday in Orlando is 9:00am in Los Angeles.

Top Tip: Set your watch as soon as you arrive in Florida so that you do not miss your ongoing transport connections. It is also essential to making sure you do not miss dining and Fastpass+ reservations. If taking a flight across time zones, set your watch straight after boarding.

Can I re-enter a park on the same day after I leave?
Sure. Walk out of the park (no need to touch your MagicBand or park ticket) and scan your MagicBand or park ticket as normal on the way in. You will still only use one day of admission.

Stroller rentals:
Strollers, also known as buggies or pushchairs, can be rented at the entrance to the four theme parks. A single stroller, recommended for children of 50lbs of less, is $15 per day, or $13 as part of a multi-day purchase. A double stroller for children of 100lbs or less is priced at $31 per day, or $27 as part of a multi-day purchase. Strollers must be returned on the same day and cannot leave the theme parks. You can use the same receipt to receive multiple strollers throughout all four theme parks on the same day. Strollers can also be rented at Disney Springs.

CAST MEMBER INSIGHT

The author says: "When parking strollers, be sure to use the designed stroller parking areas; these are generally where all the other strollers are parked. If your stroller is not in a designed stroller parking area, Cast Members will move it.

Even in stroller parking areas, strollers are moved by Cast Members to organize the layout better. Do not simply assume that a stroller has been taken if it is not exactly where you left it, look around first. Do not use bike locks to attach your stroller to poles or railings – these are a fire hazard and your stroller may be removed by security."

Useful Phone Numbers

- **Main Street USA Barber Shop Appointments:** 407-824-6550
- **Central Lost and Found:** 407-824-4245
- **Central Reservations Office (CRO):** 407-934-7639
- **Disney Dining Reservations:** 407-WDW-DINE
- **Main Disney Switchboard:** 407-824-2222
- **Firework Cruises:** 407-939-7529
- **Golf:** 407-WDW-GOLF
- **Guest Services Mail Order:** 407-363-6200
- **Kennel:** 407-824-6568
- **Resort Medical Care:** 407-648-9234
- **Recreation:** 407-WDW-PLAY
- **Reservations:** 407-934-7639
- **Tours:** 407-WDW-TOUR
- **Walt Disney World Florist and Gift Basket Department:** 407-827-3505 (disneyflorist.com)
- **Walt Disney World Transportation:** 407-824-4321
- **WDW Operation Information** (Hours etc.): 407-WDW-INFO

To dial the USA from international locations, you will need to add '001' or '+1' before these phone numbers.

Height Restrictions

Although we cover height restrictions throughout the parks section of this travel guide, this section gives you an overview of all the rides your child may or may not be able to experience.

Under no circumstances should you try and fraudulently increase the apparent height of your child through heels or other measures. Attractions Cast Members can, and will, ask for these to be removed before measuring.

Height restrictions are in place for the safety of all guests. No exceptions are made.

- **Alien Swirling Saucers** – Disney's Hollywood Studios – 32 inches (0.81m)
- **Tomorrowland Speedway** – Magic Kingdom Park – 32 inches (0.81m) to ride with an adult, or 54 inches (1.37m) to drive alone.
- **Kali River Rapids** – Animal Kingdom Park – 38 inches (0.97m)
- **Slinky Dog Dash** – Disney's Hollywood Studios – 38 inches (0.97m)
- **Seven Dwarfs Mine Train** – Magic Kingdom Park – 38 inches (0.97m)
- **Big Thunder Mountain Railroad** – Magic Kingdom Park - 40 inches (1.02m)
- **Splash Mountain** – Magic Kingdom Park - 40 inches (1.02m)
- **Stitch's Great Escape** – Magic Kingdom Park - 40 inches (1.02m)
- **Dinosaur** – Animal Kingdom Park – 40 inches (1.02m)
- **Star Tours** – Disney's Hollywood Studios – 40 inches (1.02m)
- **The Twilight Zone: Tower of Terror** – Disney's Hollywood Studios – 40 inches (1.02m)
- **Soarin'** – EPCOT – 40 inches (1.02m)
- **Expedition Everest** – Animal Kingdom Park – 44 inches (1.12m)
- **Mission: SPACE** – EPCOT – 44 inches (1.12m)
- **Space Mountain** – Magic Kingdom Park – 44 inches (1.12m)
- **Avatar Flight of Passage** – Animal Kingdom Park – 44 inches (1.12m)
- **Primeval Whirl** – Animal Kingdom Park – 48 inches (1.22m)
- **Rock 'n' Roller coaster** – Disney's Hollywood Studios – 48 inches (1.22m)

Additional height restrictions apply at the Disney water parks.

Chapter Twenty-Three | Spend Less Time Waiting

Spend less time in queue lines

The Walt Disney World Resort meticulously themes its queue lines but often you just want to get on the rides as quickly as possible. Without a strategy you WILL wait longer than you need to. Here are our top tips on minimizing your waits:

Disney hotel guests - At Walt Disney World Resort hotels (and select other hotels), you can take advantage of Extra Magic Hours (EMH) which get you one hours' early entry into one theme park per day, and you can stay up to two hours in another park after it has closed. Most popular attractions are open. Morning Extra Magic Hours are extremely valuable, as most people simply do not want to get up early, so you can hit many of the headline attractions in this first hour! Evening Extra Magic Hours are busier than the morning ones but ride waits are often less than 15 minutes, even for the bigger attractions.

Visit a non-EMH park – As Disney has over 30,000 on-site hotel rooms, the park that hosts evening Extra Magic Hours is often much busier than the other parks. The solution is to go to a different park during the day, and then visit the park with EMH during the extended opening hours only – this relies on you having a park hopper ticket. If you do not have access to EMHs, we recommend avoiding the parks on the day they host EMHs as they are busy with no extra benefit to you.

Use the Character Breakfast entrance at park opening – Look for the entrances marked "Character Breakfast". These are reserved for those who are eating in-park character breakfasts until park opening. After the other touch points start operating, these are open to everyone!

See our guide to the less busy times – If you are going on New Year's Day, expect to queue for a lot longer than in the middle of September. If you are going on a weekend expect to wait more than on a weekday. Check out our section on when to visit and find the best time for you.

The Parks Open Early – Get to the theme parks 30 minutes before the published opening time as parks regularly open before the official time.

Magic Kingdom Park opens 1 hour before the scheduled opening time. You will be kept roped off in front of Cinderella Castle until the park's opening show plays. You able to explore Main Street, U.S.A. and Town Square during this time.

Epcot frequently opens its gates 15 minutes or more before its official opening time. Not all rides will be running straight away, but the bigger ones generally are. This is a great way to get some early rides in.

Disney's Hollywood Studios opens its gates at least 15 minutes before the official opening time. On busy days, the park can open up to 45 minutes early. Attractions may or may not be operational straight away.

At *Disney's Animal Kingdom Park*, guests are usually allowed into the park 30 to 45 minutes before the published opening time. Kilimanjaro Safaris, Expedition Everest and Avatar Flight of Passage are usually operational soon after this time.

Do the popular rides first – If you are there at park opening, you can often ride several of the top attractions within just an hour! Be sure to head to these first in the listed order.
• Magic Kingdom Park: Seven Dwarfs Mine Train, Peter Pan's Flight, Space Mountain, Big Thunder Mountain, and Splash Mountain.
• Epcot: Test Track, Soarin' and Mission: Space.
• Disney's Hollywood Studios: Slinky Dog Dash, Toy Story Midway Mania, Rock n' Roller coaster and The Twilight Zone: Tower of Terror.
• Disney's Animal Kingdom Park: Avatar Flight of Passage, Na'vi River Journey, Expedition Everest, Kilimanjaro Safaris, Kali River Rapids and Dinosaur.

Post-firework riding – This mainly applies to Magic Kingdom Park but can sometimes apply to other parks too. Check what time the nighttime show is performed. If the park remains open after the show, then you can keep riding attractions until the park closes. At night, queues should be minimal or non-existent. If you fancy a last minute ride, just make sure you are in the queue line before park closing and you will get to ride!

Ride outdoor rides during the rain – Outside attractions such as Dumbo, Aladdin's Flying Carpets, Splash Mountain and Big Thunder Mountain have significantly shorter queues when it is raining than when it is not. You may get soaked, but your wait will be shorter! If there is a thunderstorm, outdoor attractions temporarily stop operation.

Top Tip: If a ride is unavailable for weather or technical reasons, many people will leave the queue. If you hang around, you can wait until the queue line reopens and jump right in! You can tell if an attraction is operational by looking at the electronic wait time sign by the entrance. If it turns off, then the attraction is not operating. Some people will stay in the queue line during storms, so there will be people ahead of you even if you join the queue as the attraction reopens.

Go shopping at the start or end of the day – Even when the park is officially closed in the evening, shops on Main Street, U.S.A. in Magic Kingdom, and other major shops in the other theme parks stay open until all guests have left. Or, do your shopping at Disney Springs on a different day! Better yet, if you are staying on-site, visit your resort hotel's own Disney store – these are usually open late. Do not waste time during the day shopping.

Chapter Twenty-Four | Guided Tours

Guided Tours

If you want to get a different perspective on the Walt Disney World Resort, consider taking one of the many guided tours on offer. Go behind the scenes at the theme parks, scuba dive or go on a private safari.

If you want a guide to take you around the parks, bypass the queues and organize your day, consider the VIP Tour Guide experience which we also cover in this section.

Backstage Magic – $275 per person (7 hours)
Pull back the curtain and discover the heritage, secrets and daily operations of Walt Disney World. At Epcot, explore the inner workings of *The American Adventure*, the patriotic Audio-Animatronics extravaganza. At Magic Kingdom Park discover hidden details on Main Street, U.S.A., and navigate the legendary underground "Utilidoor" tunnels. At Disney's Hollywood Studios learn how Imagineers thrill on *The Twilight Zone: Tower of Terror*, and visit Creative Costuming to see how Disney shows come to life.

Visit Central Shops and meet skilled craftspeople; Disney's Wilderness Lodge for a complimentary family-style barbeque lunch at Whispering Canyon Café, and the Walt Disney World Nursery & Tree Farm to learn about the botanical side of the resort. Bus transportation is provided. Guests must be 16 years of age or older.

Backstage Tales – Disney's Animal Kingdom – $90 per person (3 hours 45 minutes)
Learn about the unique challenges involved in helping Disney's animals thrive. Explore backstage animal-housing areas, and the Animal Nutrition Center and see how over 4 tons of food are prepared and distributed each day, tour the state-of-the-art veterinary hospital, and learn how Disney promotes global wildlife conservation and animal well-being. Guests must be 12 years of age or older.

Behind the Seeds – Epcot - $16 child / $20 adult (1 hour)
This tour of the fish farm and four greenhouses in The Land Pavilion is perfect for anyone with an interest in gardening or natural sciences. Visit a fish farm during feeding time and see American alligators, release ladybugs into a greenhouse, see gigantic fruits and vegetables and unusual crops from around the world and discover the latest plant-growing techniques.

Disney's The Magic Behind Our Steam Trains Tour – Magic Kingdom – $54 per person (3 hours)
On this eye-opening 3-hour tour sure to delight railroad enthusiasts, you will ride the rails around the park in a fully restored antique freight train, gain exclusive backstage access to the roundhouse, where the steam engines are stored and serviced, discover what it takes to keep these turn-of-the-century trains in top working order, and hear about Walt Disney's lifelong passion for steam trains.

Guided Tours

Disney Family Culinary Adventure – $175 per adult & $125 child (ages 9 to 12)
This tour whisks guests backstage at Disney's Contemporary Resort for a fun, interactive evening that includes time with Disney chefs, hands-on cooking and a festive, five-course dinner.

Aimed at guests 9 and older, the evening starts with an introduction to the massive catering kitchen. Guests put on aprons, hats and gloves and are divided into cooking groups and move from station to station. The stations are: Garde manger, sushi, boucherie, pasta and patisserie. Then, it's time to eat as each course is served.

Disney's Family Magic Tour – Magic Kingdom – $34 per person (2 hours)
Take off on a guided scavenger hunt collecting a series of clues as an unforgettable adventure magically unfolds around you. Follow your guide as you make way through Magic Kingdom Park, picking up clue after clue while unlocking a memorable quest. This adventure is best suited for Guests 4 to 10 years of age. Guests 16 years of age and under must be accompanied by a paying adult.

Disney's Dolphins in Depth – Epcot – $206 per person (3 hours)
Talk to the expert trainers and researchers who work with Epcot's bottlenose dolphins daily. Gain a better understanding and greater appreciation of these creatures as you interact with dolphins in waist-deep water for 30 minutes, see how Disney cares for the dolphins day to day, view backstage areas and learn how the dolphins are trained.

You do not need to swim or be SCUBA-certified. You will not swim with dolphins. Guests must be 13 years of age or older. All participants under 18 years of age must be accompanied by a paying adult.

Epcot DiveQuest – $186 per person (3 hours)
Take the plunge at the 5.7-million-gallon saltwater aquarium at Epcot, and swim with over 6,000 sea creatures. Clear waters and the absence of currents afford you amazing views of dolphins, rays and sharks.

The pavilion's giant windows make it possible for family and friends to view your dive. You will spend about 40 minutes of the tour on the actual dive. You will also tour the massive backstage infrastructure that filters and maintains this vast manmade ocean. All guests must be SCUBA-certified and 10 years of age or older. Guests 10 to 12 years old must be accompanied by a paying adult.

Epcot Seas Aqua Tour – $140 per person (2.5 hours)
Explore Caribbean Coral Reef, a 5.7-million-gallon manmade saltwater ocean. Offering a chance to snorkel for guests who are not SCUBA-certified, this tour includes about 30 minutes of actual snorkeling time.

You will also tour backstage; learn about the beautiful sea creatures through a video presentation and receive a complimentary photo of yourself in your dive gear. All snorkeling equipment is provided. Guests under 12 must be accompanied by a paying adult.

Guided Tours

Escape to Walt's Wilderness – $109 per person (5 hours)
Begin with a boat tour from the Contemporary Resort as your guide shares stories of Walt Disney and his passion for the nature. Along the way, wildlife guides and binoculars help spot the wildlife. On arrival at Fort Wilderness, a bonfire and camp-style breakfast awaits.

A wagon ride is next, followed by an archery lesson, and then a hike in the woods with surprises. The tour is recommended for ages 7 and up.

Disney's Holiday D-Lights – $259 per person (5 hours)
Celebrate the magic of the holidays with the festive sights and sounds of the season. At Epcot witness the Candlelight Processional, and at Magic Kingdom Park take in the charm of delightful holiday trimmings on Main Street, U.S.A. and behold Cinderella Castle, transformed into an ice palace for the holidays. You will meet the team responsible for turning the entire Resort into a winter wonderland. A light holiday-themed buffet is also included with your tour. This tour is offered on select nights in November and December. Guests must be 16 years of age or older.

Keys to the Kingdom Tour – Magic Kingdom – $99 per person (5 hours)
Uncover the hidden secrets of classic attractions, access the underground "Utilidoor" tunnels, discover little-known facts, trivia and other exciting tidbits about the park, explore the parade floats storage area, and enjoy your choice of lunch entrée at Columbia Harbour House, included with your tour. Valid theme park admission is required. Photography is strictly prohibited. Guests must be 16 years of age or older.

Savor the Savannah: Evening Safari Experience – $169 per person (2 hours)
Your safari begins with a journey deep into the heart of the Harambe Wildlife Reserve. You'll soon find yourself within one of the most secluded and breathtaking private viewing areas the Savannah has to offer. While savoring the Savannah scenery, you're invited to indulge in a sampling of African-inspired tapas too, paired with regional beer and wine.

Sense of Africa – $250 per person (3.5 hours)
A typical tour begins with a unique twist on breakfast at Boma -Flavors of Africa, followed by encounters with animals such as okapi, giraffe, ostriches and red river hogs. Sense of Africa is a feast for all five senses.

Animal Kingdom Lodge Starlight Safari – $70 per person (1 hour)
Climb aboard a sturdy, open-sided safari vehicle with night vision goggles to make the most of your animal-viewing extravaganza. From gazelles and giraffes to ostriches and zebras, prepare yourself for a few all-new memories as you discover different kinds of animal activity at each stop. You will even get a chance to see the inner-workings of the hotels, including their animal-friendly Cast Members!

The Ultimate Day of Thrills (6 to 7 hours) and The Ultimate Day for Young Families (6 to 7 hours) – $299 per person

These are two separate tours include experiencing a certain number of attractions such as Seven Dwarfs Mine Train, Toy Story Midway Mania! and Expedition Everest. The Ultimate Day for Young Families – A VIP Tour Experience offers attractions that are specifically accessible to young children. Both tours include a meal at a Table Service restaurant.

The UnDISCOVERed Future World – $64 per person (4 hours)

Gain insight on Walt's dream of building the Experimental Prototype Community of Tomorrow (Epcot), a living, breathing home to permanent residents and a model for city planning. Hear the story of the groundbreaking construction project that brought Epcot to life. Learn how each pavilion and its attractions are a testament to man's accomplishments and challenges. And see how Walt's legacy lives on.

You will also go backstage and visit the VIP lounge at The Seas with Nemo & Friends pavilion; walk beneath the outdoor portion of *Test Track*; head to the Cast Services building, where you can glimpse inside the wardrobe department and go behind-the-scenes at *IllumiNations: Reflections of Earth*. Valid Park Admission is required. Guests must be at least 16 years of age.

Walt Disney: Marceline to Magic Kingdom Tour – $35 per person (3 hours)

On this walking tour, discover the secrets behind the magic. Your guide will share little-known facts about Walt, as well as the design and operation of classic attractions. This insider's look at the history of Magic Kingdom Park is perfect for the avid Disney fan and offers a lighter alternative to the more in-depth Keys to the Kingdom tour.

This tour is more suited for adults, although guests as young as 12 may attend. Guests under 18 must be accompanied by a paying adult. Valid theme park admission is required.

Wild Africa Trek – Disney's Animal Kingdom – $189 per person (3 hours)

The perfect opportunity to explore the Safi River Valley and discover animals of nearly every variety in an uninhibited, natural environment. See hippos and crocodiles ten feet below as you make your way across a shaky rope bridge, secured to an overhead track with a harness. Ride in a rugged safari vehicle over an open savannah teeming with native African creatures—from giraffes to rhinos.

On your journey, your knowledgeable guide will share insights on the majestic animals, as well as the general operation of Disney's Animal Kingdom. A trained photographer will take digital pictures throughout the adventure – a complimentary service. After working up an appetite, indulge in some African-inspired snacks as well.

Guests under 18 years of age must be accompanied by a participating adult. Valid Park Admission is required. Complimentary lockers are provided.

Guided Tours

Wilderness Back Trail Adventure – $96 per person (2 hours)
Take in Florida's natural beauty while gliding along scenic back roads. Navigate a variety of surfaces from paved paths to woodland trails as you complete a 2-hour circuit that includes stops at Disney's Wilderness Lodge, the stables of Tri-Circle-D Ranch, and Bay Lake. Your guide will share trivia and anecdotes along the way. Riders must weigh between 100 and 250 pounds to participate and be in good general health. Guests must be 16 years of age or older.

Disney's Yuletide Fantasy – Magic Kingdom – $148 (3 hours 30 minutes)
On this festive and fact-filled tour, you will meet the "elves" who create the decorations for the theme parks and hotels; explore World Showcase and hear how holidays are celebrated around the globe; get an up-close look at the traditional trimmings of Main Street, U.S.A; and visit a hotel to learn how the holiday atmosphere is created. This tour is offered only on select dates in November and December. Guests must be 16 years of age or older.

Tour reservations and cancellations:
Reservations are strongly recommended for all tours and for most of them are a requirement. These can be made up to 90 days in advance. Call 407-WDW-TOUR to book. You will forfeit the entire price of your tour if you no-show or cancel within 2 days of your reservation. For VIP Tours if you cancel within this time, the cancellation fee will be 2 hours at the booked rate. The phone number to call to book VIP Tours is 407-560-4033.

Additional tour notes:
The itinerary, content, duration and availability of tours are subject to change without notice. If your tour travels backstage, no cameras, video equipment or cell phones may be used during that portion of the tour. Photography is allowed and encouraged in non-backstage areas.

VIP Tour Services

With the help of your own VIP Tour Guide, enjoy maximum fun with minimal fuss – and the Disney vacation of a lifetime.

The team at Disney's VIP Tour Services will plan the most efficient, enjoyable way for your group (up to 10 people) to see and do what's on your list. Just tell Disney what you want, and they will create your ideal itinerary!

Your VIP Tour Guide meets you at your door in a private vehicle and whisks you to the park of your choice. You will enjoy: a flexible start time of your choosing; visits to multiple theme parks in a day, if desired; the ability to experience some of your favorite attractions efficiently, even repeatedly; VIP seating for parades, select stage shows and nighttime spectaculars; shared insight from your highly knowledgeable VIP Tour Guide throughout your tour, and a completely customized experience based on your preferences.

VIP Tour Pricing:
The pricing of a VIP tour varies between $425 and $625 per hour, depending on the season. Disney recommends booking at least 72 hours in advance and you may reserve your VIP Tour up to 90 days prior. VIP Tours have a minimum duration of 6 hours and your party may include up to 10 people. Parties larger than 10 require more than one guide.

2019 Seasonal Events

There is always something unique at the Walt Disney World Resort. With everything from marathons to food tasting and floral exhibits, there is something for everyone. The main period where the entire resort is "standard" with no special events is during the summer period of June through the end of August.

Walt Disney World Marathon - Jan 9 to Jan 13, 2019

This annual event features a 26.2-mile adventure race through all four Disney theme parks – Magic Kingdom Park, Epcot, Disney's Hollywood Studios and Disney's Animal Kingdom. There is also a half marathon. Also included in the weekend is 'Goofy's Race and a Half Challenge,' which combines Saturday's half marathon and Sunday's full marathon for 39.3 miles of fun.

There is also a 5km run, the Walt Disney World 10K, and the Dopey Challenge, where participants run the 5K, 10K, half marathon and marathon (48.6 miles over the course of 4 days).

Epcot International Festival of the Arts - Jan 18 to Feb 25, 2019

At the Epcot International Festival of the Arts you can explore the visual arts with galleries, workshops and seminars. Then try new food with the culinary arts. Finally, enjoy performing arts from acrobatics to living statues.

A collaboration with Disney Theatrical brings an exciting new showcase of favorite music and Broadway talent to the America Gardens Theatre stage every 2 weeks.

Disney's Princess Half Marathon Weekend - Feb 21 to Feb 24, 2019

This predominantly women's Half Marathon brings guests of all ages together to celebrate all the qualities a princess possesses.

The weekend features a two-day health and fitness expo geared towards women, a family fun run of 5km and kids' races.

Guests can also run the Disney Enchanted 10K, and the Glass Slipper Challenge, where participants run the 10K and half marathon over the course of 2 days.

Atlanta Braves Spring Training - Feb 25 to Mar 23, 2019

The Atlanta Braves have made it a staple part of their training to visit Disney's Wide World of Sports Complex for Spring training. 2019 will be the last time they do this, so turn up to see the magic for one last time.

Star Wars Rival Run Weekend - Apr 4 to Apr 7, 2019

Runners who join the Galactic Empire will enjoy a true Star Wars experience, including Dark side-inspired medals and merchandise throughout the weekend.

This event includes a 5K, 10K, kids races, and half marathon, plus a special challenge for completing the 10K and half marathon called the Star Wars Rival Run Challenge!

Seasonal Events

Epcot International Flower & Garden Festival - Mar 6 to Jun 3, 2019

Future World and World Showcase bloom with more than 30 million colorful blossoms, interactive garden activities for kids and workshops with national gardening experts during this annual spring festival at Epcot.

While exploring the themed gardens, guests can taste sweets and savories from about a dozen food-and-beverage marketplaces surrounding the World Showcase Lagoon. Plus, musical entertainment pairs perfectly with brilliant botanicals during a complimentary concert.

Disney gardeners lead weekend how-to Gardening Seminars at the Festival Center, where guests also can pick up signature festival merchandise.

When the sun sets, illuminated topiary and play gardens glow brightly for an after-dark festival experience.

Mickey's Not-So-Scary Halloween Party - 2019 dates TBC

A family-friendly fright-fest in Magic Kingdom Park featuring a parade, trick-or-treating throughout the park, face painting, and more.

You can expect: a Villains show on the Castle Forecourt stage; a dead barbershop quartet in Frontierland; and Mickey's "Boo-to-You" Halloween Parade with the Headless Horseman. The night wouldn't be complete without 'Happy HalloWishes', a ghoulish firework display when The Ghost Host from the Haunted Mansion and notorious Disney Villains light up the sky to remixes of their favorite songs.

Mickey's Not-So-Scary Halloween Party also features treat trails where more candy is given out per

guest than we could eat in an entire year.

In 2018, Mickey's Not-So-Scary Halloween Parties are held from 7:00pm to midnight in August (17, 24, 28, 31), September (3, 7, 9, 11, 14, 16, 18, 21, 23, 25, 28, 30) and October (2, 4, 5, 8, 9, 11, 12, 14, 16, 18, 19, 21, 23, 25, 26, 28, 30, 31).

This party is a separate ticketed event from standard park admission. Ticket prices in 2016 start at $75 per adult and $70 per child, and rise to $125 and $120 respectively, excluding tax. Peak date nights are more expensive than non-peak nights. Tickets often sell out in advance and reservations are highly recommended.

2019's Halloween event will be broadly similar.

Seasonal Events

Epcot International Food & Wine Festival - 2019 dates TBC

Savor fine wines and delectable cuisine during the Epcot International Food & Wine Festival featuring live entertainment such as the 'Eat to the Beat' concert series, guest chefs, culinary demonstrations, seminars and more.

Festival highlights include: 35 international food and beverage marketplaces; signature dining experiences with world-renowned chefs; exciting culinary demonstrations and beverage seminars; the Eat to the Beat concert series; more than 270 chefs including Disney chefs and culinary stars; and the Party for the Senses grand tasting

events on Saturday evenings.

With so much to see and do, you can come back to the festival again and again and discover something new each time!

Most of the festival entertainment is included in regular park admission. Food and drink is an extra charge. There are over 250 food-and-beverage items — each tapas-sized portion or drink is priced at $4 to $10.

Disney Wine & Dine Half Marathon - Oct 31 to Nov 3, 2019

The ultimate "Runners' Night Out" features a half marathon. After finishing, runners and their guests can celebrate their accomplishment at an exclusive after hours' party. The weekend also includes kids' races, a 5K family fun run, and a health and fitness expo.

Mickey's Very Merry Christmas Party - 2019 dates TBC

This party allows guests to delight in some holiday cheer on select evenings throughout November and December. This is an extra-ticketed event.

As well as being able to experience the attractions throughout the park and meet characters, there are extra exclusive party-only experiences.

During the party, guests can experience: the castle sparkling with thousands of white lights; Mickey's Once Upon A Christmastime Parade featuring classic Disney characters, elves, toy soldiers and even Santa

himself; Holiday Wishes, a breath-taking music and fireworks show; A Totally Tomorrowland Christmas; the Mickey's Most Merriest Celebration Show; A Frozen Holiday Wish castle

lighting; snowfall on Main Street, U.S.A. and much more! Guests also get complimentary hot cocoa and cookies all night long.

Adult prices are $99 to $125,

Seasonal Events

and child tickets are priced at $94 to $120. Tax is extra.

Party dates for 2018 are: November (8, 9, 12, 13, 15, 16, 25, 27, 29, 30) and December (2, 4, 6, 7, 9, 11, 13, 14, 16, 18, 20, 21). Some dates above incur an additional surcharge of up to $8 per ticket.

From December 22nd 2018 inclusive all the entertainment from the party will be available to all guests without needing to buy a separate ticket for the party (it will simply be included in regular theme park admission). However, if you do wait until December 22nd 2018, expect the parks to be very busy and hotel room prices at their peak. The 2019 event will be broadly similar.

Holiday Events – Magic Kingdom, Resorts, Animal Kingdom, Hollywood Studios and Disney Springs - November & December

Walt Disney World Resort is all aglitter during the Holiday season with dazzling lights, spirited song and even snow flurries.

Here's what is in store: the Mickey's Very Merry Christmas Party at Magic Kingdom (an extra ticketed event); Candlelight Processional at Epcot (included in theme park admission); plus, caroling, tree lighting ceremonies, decorations, and visits by Santa, included in your theme park admission.

Most details over these next pages have not yet been confirmed to be returning in 2019, but event details are broadly similar year on year.

Magic Kingdom Park:
At the Magic Kingdom, guests can expect a Holiday version of the Jungle Cruise entitled "Jingle Cruise" with a revised script and new décors overlaid on the existing attraction.

What's more, Santa's elves have transformed the Magic Kingdom into a winter wonderland with festive wreaths, bows, garlands, sparkling lights, parades and towering Christmas trees.

The fun includes the 'Holiday Wishes' nighttime fireworks spectacular, plus Disney characters all dressed up for the holidays.

Also at Magic Kingdom Park, during a live show Cinderella Castle is transformed in a glistening ice palace for the holidays — thanks to a special effects spectacle bathing the castle in 200,000 shimmering white lights. Magic Kingdom guests are treated nightly to the dramatic "Frozen Holiday Wish" celebration.

Additionally, from December 22nd 2018 inclusive, "Mickey's Once Upon a Christmastime Parade" is presented to day guests in the park in place of Festival of Fantasy Parade.

The Resorts:
At Fort Wilderness Resort and Campground, you can enjoy a holiday sleigh ride through the woodland nightly from late November to late December. Sleighs hold up to 4 adults (or two adults and 3 children). The 25-minute ride is $84.

Disney's Grand Floridian Resort is a favorite holiday stop with its 16-foot-high Victorian gingerbread house located in the lobby.

Disney's Beach Club Resort hosts an incredible gingerbread carousel display, accompanied by the smell of Christmas treats wafting through the entryway.

Disney's Contemporary Resort and Disney's

Boardwalk Resort have their own gingerbread displays.

Disney's Wilderness Lodge and Disney's Animal Kingdom Lodge showcase breathtaking Christmas trees towering inside the resorts.

Disney's Animal Kingdom:
At Disney's Animal Kingdom, meet Mickey and Minnie at Adventurers Outpost for a special photo opportunity with the duo dress in their holiday best.

Disney Springs:
At Disney Springs you can see enhanced holiday entertainment, specialty foods and festive décor. Santa will be there too, of course.

Disney's Hollywood Studios:
"Jingle Bell, Jingle BAM!" is a festive nighttime show featuring a combination of fireworks, special effects, snow, music and projections of Disney's most cherished Christmas characters on the Chinese Theater.

Sunset Seasons Greetings is another nighttime projection show featuring lots of snow.

Guests can also meet Santa Claus from November 9th to December 24th, 2018. From December 25th to December 31st, you can meet Santa Goofy instead.

New Year's Eve:
Epcot and Disney's Magic Kingdom get very busy for new Year's Eve and you can expect the parks to fill to capacity by midday, at which point no further guests will be allowed in. There is no extra cost for access on this date, but certain private events are available to book at hotels and other locations. The parks are best avoided at this time of year as they are very crowded and wait times are astronomical. The 2019 event will be broadly similar.

Epcot: International Festival of the Holidays - 2019 dates TBC

There is a lot of entertainment for the Holiday season at Epcot and it is all included with Epcot park admission.

The Candlelight Processional is a retelling of the Christmas story by a celebrity narrator who is accompanied by a 50-piece orchestra and a choir. The 2018 event runs nightly at The America Gardens Theater at Epcot from November 22nd to December 30th. It is presented three times per night at 5:00pm, 6:45pm and 8:15pm.

In 2018 the line-up of narrators includes Neil Patrick Harris, Whoopi Goldberg and Jodi Benson.

Each year, *JOYFUL! A Gospel Celebration of the Season* blends the soulful expressiveness of Gospel and inspirational music with

the sounds of jazz, R&B and urban music at the Future World Fountain Stage.

The World Showcase comes alive with the nighttime spectacular *IllumiNations: Reflections of Earth* with a unique finale celebrating the season.

Other festive Holiday offerings include a Gingerbread Village at The Land pavilion, with sweet recreations of Walt Disney World Resort's theme park icons, plenty of holiday merchandise and food and beverage offerings around World Showcase.

Guests can also celebrate each country's holiday traditions with storytellers at each pavilion during Holidays Around the World including Father Christmas at the UK Pavilion, Mr. & Mrs. Claus, Hanukkah traditions and Kwanzaa celebrations at the American Adventure and much more.

2019 and The Future...

The Walt Disney World Resort prides itself on constantly innovating and making improvements for its guests. As such, there are always new projects in progress – from new rides and shows, to new lands, parades and more. Here is just a sneak preview at what has been officially confirmed by Disney.

EPCOT: New Nighttime Spectacular

The nighttime shows at each park are the highlight of the day for many visitors and after 20 years of performances, Illuminations: Reflections of Earth will be closing in Summer 2019. An interim experience called "Epcot Forever" will debut in Fall 2019, and in 2020 the new - currently un-named - show will debut.

Epcot Forever will begin "with a spark of imagination that swells into an epic spectacle of fireworks, music, lighting, lasers, and special effects kites." whereas the new show in 2020 will feature "massive floating set pieces, custom-built LED panels, choreographed moving fountains, lights, pyrotechnics and lasers.

EPCOT: New Ride - Remy's Ratatouille Adventure

A new trackless dark ride is currently under construction Epcot's France Pavilion.

The ride is expected to be a direct clone of the same ride at Disneyland Paris.

In the ride guests will board ratmobiles and journey through Chef Remy and Chef Gusteau's kitchens in a wild adventure.

We expect a Spring or Summer 2020 opening, although no official date has been announced by Disney.

EPCOT: New Ride - Guardians of the Galaxy

A new roller coaster themed to Guardians of the Galaxy is also under construction at Epcot.

Details are still sparse at the moment but Disney has announced that the new ride will be "one of the world's longest enclosed roller coasters"

Disney has announced the ride will open in 2021.

EPCOT: Other small changes

Other Epcot projects include a Beauty and the Beast singalong show in the France pavilion, new videos for both the Canada and China pavilions, replacing the current shows, a new restaurant in Japan and a new Space Restaurant next to the Mission: SPACE attraction.

Magic Kingdom: New Ride - TRON Roller coaster

A new TRON roller coaster similar to the one built at Shanghai Disneyland is under construction at the Magic Kingdom.

Guests will sit in Lightcyles just like in the TRON movies.

The Walt Disney World railroad and The Tomorrowland Speedway will close for an extended period to facilitate the construction.

This new attraction will open by 2021.

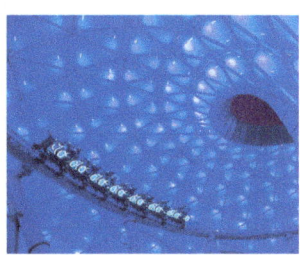

Hollywood Studios: Star Wars - Galaxy's Edge

Star Wars: Galaxy's Edge will span 14 acres and is set to open in late Fall 2019.

Based on a new planet in the Star Wars universe, Galaxy's Edge will house two new major attractions. In "Millennium Falcon: Smugglers Run" guests will take part in a secret mission. In "Star Wars: Rise of the Resistance" guests will be put face-to-face with the First Order from "The Force Awakens."

Guests will be able to shop at Black Spire's marketplace, Merchant Row and Smuggler's Row. Guests will also be able to meet characters.

Guests will be able to dine at the main restaurant -

Oga's Cantina - as well as at Docking Bay 7 and Bantha Tracks and sample unique delights such as Blue Milk.

Hollywood Studios: Mickey & Minnie's Runaway Railway

Opening in Summer 2019, Mickey & Minnie's Runaway Railway will be a brand new attraction for Disney's Hollywood Studios.

Here is how Disney describes it: "On the attraction, the fun begins when you see the premiere of a new cartoon short with Mickey and Minnie getting ready for a picnic.

As they head out, they drive alongside a train and find out that the engineer is Goofy. Then, one magical moment lets you step into the movie and on Goofy's train for a wacky, wild ride.

Mickey & Minnie's Runaway Railway will put you inside the wacky and unpredictable world of a Mickey Mouse Cartoon

Short where you're the star and anything can happen."

Other Projects

Disney's Skyliner transportation system will open in Fall 2019. Disney's Riviera Resort is expected to open in Summer 2019. Finally, a new hyper-detailed immersive Star Wars resort has been announced with no set opening date at the time of publication.

Chapter Twenty-Seven | Comparing Disney theme park resorts

Comparing the Walt Disney World Resort and the Disneyland Resort

Before Walt Disney began to dream about building the Walt Disney World Resort, he had already accomplished another dream – the creation of Disneyland in California. Opened in 1955, Disneyland was the first theme park of its kind – it was not a carnival, but a place where families could have fun together.

As many visitors may have visited Disneyland we have created this section. The two resorts are very different in scope and offerings - discover them here.

The atmosphere

Walt Disney World is the largest of the two resorts and, naturally, the atmosphere varies from place to place and park to park.

Ultimately, due to its size and the time it takes to get off-property, the larger resort is very good at keeping you in the "Disney bubble". Everywhere you go you will see Mickey-shaped road signs, perfectly shaped lawns and Disney characters. It truly is an immersive atmosphere.

Walt Disney World's Magic Kingdom does not have the charm of the Disneyland Resort, though, seeming more "fake" and oversized.

Disneyland Resort has a much quainter atmosphere to it with everything being very small compared to its Floridian friend.

However, the attractions at Disneyland Resort's parks are too close together, and walkways very often crowded.

Disneyland Resort is also the opposite of Walt Disney World – at Disneyland it is very easy to leave the atmosphere behind and step into the real world. Whether that is a positive or negative point depends on you.

Resort Size

Walt Disney World – The resort is huge, spanning 47 square miles (twice the size of Manhattan). That means Disney has room to build lakes, resort hotels, water parks and golf courses for example – the resort even has enough free land to double in size.

However, at times, the resort seems almost too big: locations often feel unnecessarily spaced out, and a 20-minute drive to get from your hotel to the Magic Kingdom can feel excessive.

Disneyland Resort – This is a tiny resort with a very intimate feel, although Disneyland Park can feel a little small and cramped in our opinion.

Everything is within walking distance, including the two parks, which are literally opposite each other. Disneyland does not have room for expansion.

Offerings

Walt Disney World has the widest offering, with four theme parks. Magic Kingdom Park, Epcot, Hollywood Studios and Animal Kingdom contain some incredibly unique attractions and themed environments, as well as some Disneyland Resort clones.

Where else can you enjoy a safari ride on Kilimanjaro Safaris, then get a bus to Epcot and fly above world monuments in Soarin', take a boat to Hollywood Studios and drop 13-stories in the Tower of Terror and finally finish off your night by taking a monorail to Magic Kingdom Park and watching the Wishes firework show in front of Cinderella Castle?

The resort has a wealth of experiences to be explored including two water parks, golf courses, dozens of resort hotels, and backstage guided tours.

Let's not forget the fact that you can take boats between resorts, go on carriage rides, sit on a beach, hire a speedboat, visit Disney Springs and much more at the Walt Disney World resort too! Walt Disney World hands down beats Disneyland Resort in terms of its offerings.

Disneyland Resort offers two theme parks with some incredible unique attractions such as *Radiator Springs Racers* and *Indiana Jones Adventure*. Outside the two theme parks, there is the Downtown Disney area with shops and dining options. There are no golf courses, no water parks and only three on-site Disney resort hotels.

Accommodation

Walt Disney World has a variety of resort hotels, with over twenty different options.

Deluxe hotels in particular have a quality that make you forget you are in Central Florida by immersing you in a different environment: you can be taken to a campsite, to the wilderness, Polynesia, Africa, the Victorian Era, the world of Pixar, New Orleans and other places.

The theming at the hotels is second to none, as are the amenities on offer. There is also something for every budget. Exceptional theming is provided in all categories

of hotel, and not just deluxe resorts!

At Disneyland Resort, only one of the hotels - the Grand Californian - really has the quality of theming that is so prevalent at Walt Disney World. The other on-site hotels seem like Hiltons with Disney branding, unfortunately.

At Disneyland Resort, there are only three hotels and they are all very expensive. Especially when you can get a much cheaper non-Disney hotel ten minutes' walk away.

Attractions

Let's face it: most people go to theme parks for the attractions - the ride and shows. You would probably not pay a theme park's daily admission price to go and eat in a restaurant, or walk around in a themed environment. Attractions are king.

Walt Disney World has a huge variety of attractions, although some of them are clones of others at the Disneyland Resort – and inferior versions at that, such as *"it's a small world"* and *Pirates of the Caribbean*.

The Florida resort does have many unique attractions though: *Expedition Everest, Mickey's Philharmagic*, interactive experiences, *Mission: SPACE, Avatar Flight of Passage* and *Test Track*. It also has different versions of *Splash, Big Thunder* and *Space Mountain*.

The World Showcase in Epcot is also composed of a multitude of incredible immersive experiences – a true testament to Disney's incredible theming.

However, we feel that Magic Kingdom Park lacks in old-style classic dark rides such as *Snow White*, though it is nice to see the *Carousel of Progress* still in operation.

Disney's Hollywood Studios feels like it lacks rides in general, and is filled with shows to pad its offerings. This park is going through a huge overhaul at the moment to correct this.

Disney's Animal Kingdom is unprecedented in scale, the attractions are incredible and this is one of our favorite Disney parks anywhere in the world.

FastPass+ is a great system at Walt Disney World allowing you to guarantee you will ride certain attractions even before you reach the park.

However, due to FastPass+, rides such as *Peter Pan's Flight* have extremely long standby waits at Walt Disney World, whereas queues lines are much more manageable at Disneyland. The parks need more attractions at Walt Disney World.

Disneyland Resort has several unique attractions such as *The Matterhorn, Finding Nemo Submarine Voyage, Indiana Jones Adventure, California Screamin', Grizzly River Run, Alice in Wonderland, Mr. Toad's Wild Ride, Monster's Inc.: Mike and Sulley to the Rescue* and *Radiator Springs Racers* to name but a few. You can also actually go inside the castle at Disneyland, unlike at Disney World.

Some attractions such as *"it's a small world", Winnie the Pooh* and *Pirates of the Caribbean* are also better than their Floridian counterparts, although *Space Mountain* is not as good here, in our opinion. The lack of *Rock 'n' Roller coaster* at the Disneyland Resort saddens us, and Florida's *Tower of Terror* is completely different. Also, the water rides here really do get you wet, unlike those in Florida. Both parks have a good number of attractions to fill a few days, and there is no weaker park at the Disneyland Resort.

The Magic and the Cast Members

The Cast Members at Walt Disney World are hugely empowered to create magic with tools such as vouchers to replace damaged or lost items.

There are also planned magical moments throughout the day such as free desserts and drinks at Quick Service locations and being able to pull the sword out of the stone by the carousel at Magic Kingdom Park – all done in a seemingly random fashion. Magic is everywhere and Cast Members are both empowered, and encouraged, to create it.

Disneyland Resort is very much like Walt Disney World. The Cast Members, however, do seems to go above and beyond to make your day special, in our experience - they will do anything possible to make your holiday or vacation an unforgettable one.

Dining

Walt Disney World has the luxury of offering many different types of food, particularly throughout its resort hotels.

You can go to Boma and get a taste of Africa, visit the countries in the World Showcase at Epcot and try Canadian, Japanese and Italian food, sample incredible tastes at Satu'li Canteen, or simply settle for simpler theme park fare. Prices are more expensive than comparable food outlets in the US, but are typical prices for a theme park.

Dining reservations start 180 days in advance and popular restaurants have to be booked as soon as reservations open to avoid disappointment.

Disneyland Resort offers significantly fewer food options than the Walt Disney World resort but has some great breakfast offerings, especially in Adventureland. The food here is more standard theme park fare (but there are some good dining experiences in the hotels too) and there are definitely fewer Table Service restaurants to eat in than at Walt Disney World.

The dining plans at Disneyland Resort also offer no money-saving value, which we feel is very disappointing. Dining reservations only open 60 days in advance, and getting these is much easier.

Entertainment

Walt Disney World – Magic Kingdom Park provides a wealth of entertainment, with dozens of character meet and greats. Unfortunately, there is only one real live 'stage show' that takes place up to five times a day in front of the castle.

Magic Kingdom offers quite a few sit-down recorded shows such as *Mickey's Philharmagic, Monster's Inc., Carousel of Progress, Hall of Presidents, Country Bear Jamboree* and *The Enchanted Tiki Room*; some are excellent but many feel dated.

Animal Kingdom Park offers the most incredible shows, followed by Disney's Hollywood Studios. Epcot's World Showcase is filled with street-mosphere (as is Hollywood Studios) and cinema-style shows too. Only Magic Kingdom Park offers a daily parade.

Nighttime entertainment is widespread throughout the parks. At Animal Kingdom guests can marvel at *Rivers of Light*, Epcot presents *Illuminations*, Magic Kingdom presents the wonderful *Happily Ever After* and Hollywood Studios presents *Fantasmic*.

Characters can be found throughout the parks but not usually 'randomly', they are usually part of scheduled meet and greets. Furthermore, there are little touches at Magic Kingdom Park such as the Trolley Show in the morning, and the unadvertised Kiss Goodnight at the end of the day. These are truly unique experiences.

All that is needed to improve the entertainment roster at the resort is more stage shows at Magic Kingdom Park, the addition of parades at the other parks, and more random character meet and greets.

Disneyland Resort has more random character appearances, incredible casting with characters who are exceptionally true to life, up to four nighttime shows in just two parks and many, many more stage shows.

The parades at the two parks are also the most creative and fun parades we have ever seen too, plus with *Fantasmic* and a fireworks show, there is a lot to see. At the other park next door you can enjoy *World of Color* too!

Miscellaneous

Disneyland Resort was clearly designed for standards of over 60 years ago. For example, the turnstiles are tiny, and accessibility is not great.

Everything does, however, seem more relaxed and natural than at Walt Disney World. You get the same quality of service just without it feeling like it is being faked by the Cast Member at the Disneyland Resort. They just seem to naturally enjoy their jobs more.

The roping off of crowds during parades and fireworks is a great way of keeping walkways clear - we were very impressed with this, and it is something that should be done at Walt Disney World too. Free Wi-Fi coverage in the parks is limited.

Walt Disney World has Free Wi-Fi in the parks, which is with excellent coverage. The weather is generally warm year-round. However, hurricane season as well as the hot, humid summers can put a downer on things.

FastPass+ can either be a godsend or not so much, depending on your preferences. Planning far, far in advance is almost compulsory here.

Overall

Disneyland Resort is the perfect resort for locals and vacationers alike and we can see why it has been so successful.

Even 60 years after opening, it still captures a truly magical era, yet the resort is not afraid of keeping up with the times.

For a resort that is a fraction of the size of Walt Disney World, it is still world class, a testament to how it has kept up with the times.

Walt Disney World is truly what it says on the tin - a world of Disney - it can be almost inescapable once you are in its claws, but in a good way.

You really do get immersed inside the Disney bubble here, and it is easy to see why it is the world's most visited tourist destination.

Ride and Attraction Comparisons

This section lists all the attractions at the Disneyland Resort and compares them to their Walt Disney World Resort counterparts, as well as listing those that are completely original. This way, if you have been to the Disneyland Resort you can best use your time.

Unique attractions at Walt Disney World:

Magic Kingdom Park – *The Barnstormer, Country Bear Jamboree, Enchanted Tales with Belle, The Hall of Presidents, The Magic Carpets of Aladdin, Monsters, Inc. Laugh Floor, Seven Dwarfs Mine Train, Sorcerers of the Magic Kingdom, Tomorrowland Transit Authority People Mover* and *Walt Disney's Carousel of Progress.*

Epcot – *The American Adventure, The Circle of Life, Disney Phineas and Ferb: Agent P's World Showcase Adventure, Ellen's Energy Adventure, Gran Fiesta Tour Starring The Three Caballeros, ImageWorks: The What-If Labs, Impressions de France, Journey into Imagination with Figment, Living with the Land, Frozen Ever After, Mission: SPACE, O Canada!, Reflections of China, The Seas with Nemo & Friends, Spaceship Earth, Innoventions* and *Test Track.*

Disney's Hollywood Studios – *Beauty and the Beast Live on Stage, Disney Junior, Indiana Jones Epic Stunt Spectacular!, Rock 'n' Roller Coaster: Starring Aerosmith, Star Tours: The Adventures Continue, Voyage of the Little Mermaid, The Twilight Zone: Tower of Terror* and *Walt Disney Presents.*

Disney's Animal Kingdom – *Dinosaur, Discovery Island Trails, Expedition Everest, Finding Nemo: The Musical, It's Tough to be a Bug!, Kali*

River Rapids, Kilimanjaro Safaris, Maharajah Jungle Trek, Gorilla Falls Exploration Trail, Primeval Whirl, TriceraTop Spin, Flight of Passage, Na'vi River Journey, Wildlife Express Train and Festival of the Lion King.

Attractions that are the same at both resorts:
• Enchanted Tiki Room
• Frontierland Shootin'

Attractions at both resorts but with some differences:
• *Astro Orbiter* – The Disneyland version is on the ground
• *Autopia* – The Disneyland version has nicer theming.
• *Big Thunder Mountain Railroad* – Similar in style to the Disneyland version, but Disneyland's has better special effects.
• *Buzz Lightyear Astro Blasters* – Disneyland's is better because of the different layout and more interactive guns.
• *Disneyland Railroad* – The Disneyland version has more stops and is grander than at Walt Disney World.
• *Dumbo the Flying Elephant* – The Walt Disney World version has a fun queue for kids and lower wait times with its two sets of Dumbos.
• *Haunted Mansion* – Different facade and one scene is missing in the Disneyland version. Florida's does not get a Halloween and Christmas makeover like it does at Disneyland.
• *"it's a small world"* – Very similar inside but we prefer the Disneyland version due to the inclusion of subtle Disney characters. The attraction also gets a Holiday Exposition
• *King Arthur Carousel*
• *The Little Mermaid: Ariel's Undersea Adventure* – The queue at Walt Disney World is much better but there is never a wait at the Disneyland Resort, whereas waits can top 45 minutes at Walt Disney World.
• *Mad Tea Party*
• *The Many Adventures of Winnie the Pooh* – Add narration at Disneyland,

overlay, which it does not in Florida.
• *Jungle Cruise* – The scenes are reordered, and there is an indoor section at Walt Disney World. It is largely the same experience.
• *Main Street Vehicles* – Different vehicles.
• *Mickey's House and Meet Mickey* – This exists at Disneyland but in a different format, the queue at Disneyland is more fun through Mickey's house. However, Mickey talks in Walt Disney World, which makes us prefer the Floridian version of this attraction.
• *Peter Pan's Flight* – Shares many scenes and the ride experience is very similar. The Walt Disney World version has FastPass+.
• *Tom Sawyer Island* plus there is rarely a wait. Walt Disney world has a better queue line.
• *Mark Twain Riverboat*
• *MuppetVision 3D*
• *Soarin'* – Different queues.
• *Star Tours: The Adventures Continue*
• *Toy Story Midway Mania* – Walt Disney World's version has Fastpass+. The queue line is different too.
• *Turtle Talk with Crush*

• *Pirates of the Caribbean* – There is only one drop in the Walt Disney World version and the scenes are different. It is also a much shorter ride. You usually won't get wet in Orlando, and Orlando's *Pirates* has FastPass+.
• *Space Mountain* – Different ride layout and storyline. The Walt Disney World version has more drops and is more exciting, but Disneyland's is arguably better themed. Disneyland also gets Halloween and Star Wars overlays; Florida's version doesn't.
• *Splash Mountain* – This ride is shorter at Disneyland but you usually get absolutely soaked compared with Walt Disney World's version. The storyline and the interiors are laid out differently, but are similar.

A Special Thanks

Thank you very much for reading our travel guide to Walt Disney World. We hope that we have made a big difference to your vacation and you have found some tips that will save you time and money! Remember to take this guide with you while you are on vacation and use it in the parks.

If you have any questions or feedback us, please use the 'Contact Us' section on our website at www.independentguidebooks.com/

If you have enjoyed this guide, you will want to check out:
• The Independent Guide to Universal Orlando
• The Independent Guide to Universal Studios Hollywood
• The Independent Guide to Disneyland
• The Independent Guide to Disneyland Paris
• The Independent Guide to Paris
• The Independent Guide to London
• The Independent Guide to New York City
• The Independent Guide to Hong Kong
• The Independent Guide to Tokyo
• The Independent Guide to Dubai

Have a magical day!

Photo credits:
The following photos have been used under a Creative Commons license.

Anna Fox for Test Track; Benjamin Esham for Illuminations; Darren Wittko for photos of Animal Kingdom Lodge, and Pirates of the Caribbean; Daryl Mitchell for Pop Century; Darryl Kenyon for Kali River Rapids; d.k.peterson (Flickr user) for Disney Princess Half Marathon; Mark & Paul Luukkonen for Princess Fairytale Hall, Canada Pavilion and The Barnstormer; 'Flickr mjurn' for Old Key West; Greg Goebel for Astro Orbiter; Harshlight (Flickr user) for photos of Mad Tea Party, Seven Dwarfs Mine Train and Peter Pan's Flight; Inzakira (Flickr user) for Living with the Land; Jeff Kays for Blizzard Beach, Buzz Lightyear Space Ranger Spin and Soarin; Joseph Brent for ESPN Wide World of Sports; Justin Ennis for Jungle Cruise; Kyosuke Takayama for Norway Pavilion; Leigh Caldwell for the Halloween Party photo; Lou Oms for Imagination Pavilion; Luis Brizzante for Holiday Wishes and Spaceship Earth; Matthew Freeman for Splash Mountain; Michael Gray for photos of Mickey's Philharmagic, Monster's Inc, Stitch's Great Escape, Caribbean Beach resort, Epcot Food and Wine festival, Holiday Splendor, and Club Cool; Michelle Tribe for Coronado Springs; Paul Hudson for Disney Springs and Mexico Pavilion; 'Paula and Cathy' for Turtle Talk; Phil Whitehouse for Cinderella Castle, in Fantasyland Section of guide; QuesterMark (Flickr user) for Contemporary Resort; Rhys A for Beach Club; rickpilot_2000 (Flickr user) for Typhoon Lagoon and Dinosaur; Sam Howzit for The Many Adventures of Winnie the Pooh, Very Merry Christmas Party, Big Thunder Mountain and it's a small world; Sonja - Epcot Holidays around the World; Wikimedia for Primeval Whirl and Flower and Garden Festival; zannaland (Flickr user) for Sorcerer's of the Magic Kingdom and The Barnstomer; Big Front Page Image - Phillie Casablanca, Back Castle at night photo - Frank H Phillips; Sorcerers of the Magic Kingdom - zannaland; Tom Sawyer Island - Chad Sparkes; Philharmagic - Sam Howzit; Turtle Talk with Crush, Jedi Training, Triceratop Spin - Theme Park Tourist; Voyage of the Little Mermaid - Loren Javier; Walt Disney Presents, Epcot Festival of the Arts - Harshlight; Indiana Jones - Thomas Jung; Gorilla - Corey Ann; "it all started with a mouse" - Disney Parks Blog; Up! A Great Bird Aventure - Joel (coconut wireless); Na'vi River Journey - mliu92; and Lego Store - mrice1996;

Park Maps

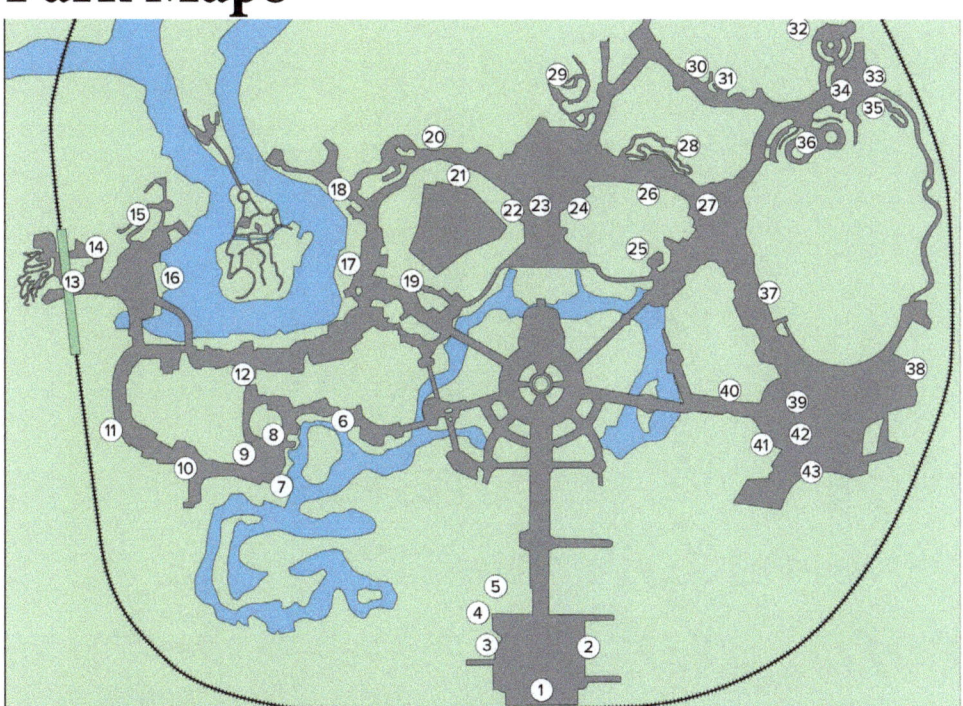

Magic Kingdom Park Attractions

1. Walt Disney World Railroad Main Street, U.S.A. Station
2. Town Square Theatre (FP+)
3. City Hall
4. Sorcerer's of the Magic Kingdom
5. Harmony Barber Shop
6. Swiss Family Treehouse
7. Jungle Cruise (FP+)
8. The Magic Carpets of Aladdin FP+
9. Walt Disney's Enchanted Tiki Room
10. Pirates of the Caribbean (FP+)
11. A Pirate's Adventure – Treasures of the Seven Seas
12. Country Bear Jamboree
13. Splash Mountain (FP+)
14. Walt Disney World Railroad Frontierland Station
15. Big Thunder Mountain Railroad (FP+)
16. Tom Sawyer Island
17. Liberty Square Riverboat
18. Haunted Mansion (FP+)
19. The Hall of Presidents
20. "it's a small world"
21. Peter Pan's Flight (FP+)
22. Mickey's Philharmagic (FP+)
23. Prince Charming Regal Carousel
24. Princess Fairytale Hall (FP+)
25. Fairytale Garden
26. The Many Adventures of Winnie the Pooh (FP+)
27. Mad Tea Party (FP+)
28. Seven Dwarfs Mine Train (FP+)
29. Enchanted Tales with Belle (FP+)
30. Under the Sea – Journey of the Little Mermaid (FP+)
31. Ariel's Grotto (FP+)
32. Pete's Silly Sideshow
33. Walt Disney World Railroad Fantasyland Station
34. Casey Jr. Splash 'n' Soak
35. The Barnstormer (FP+)
36. Dumbo the Flying Elephant (FP+)
37. Tomorrowland Speedway (FP+)
38. Space Mountain (FP+)
39. Astro Orbiter
40. Monster's Inc. Laugh Floor (FP+)
41. Buzz Lightyear's Space Ranger Spin (FP+)
42. Tomorrowland Transit Authority
43. Walt Disney's Carousel of Progress

Chapter Twenty-Nine | Park Maps

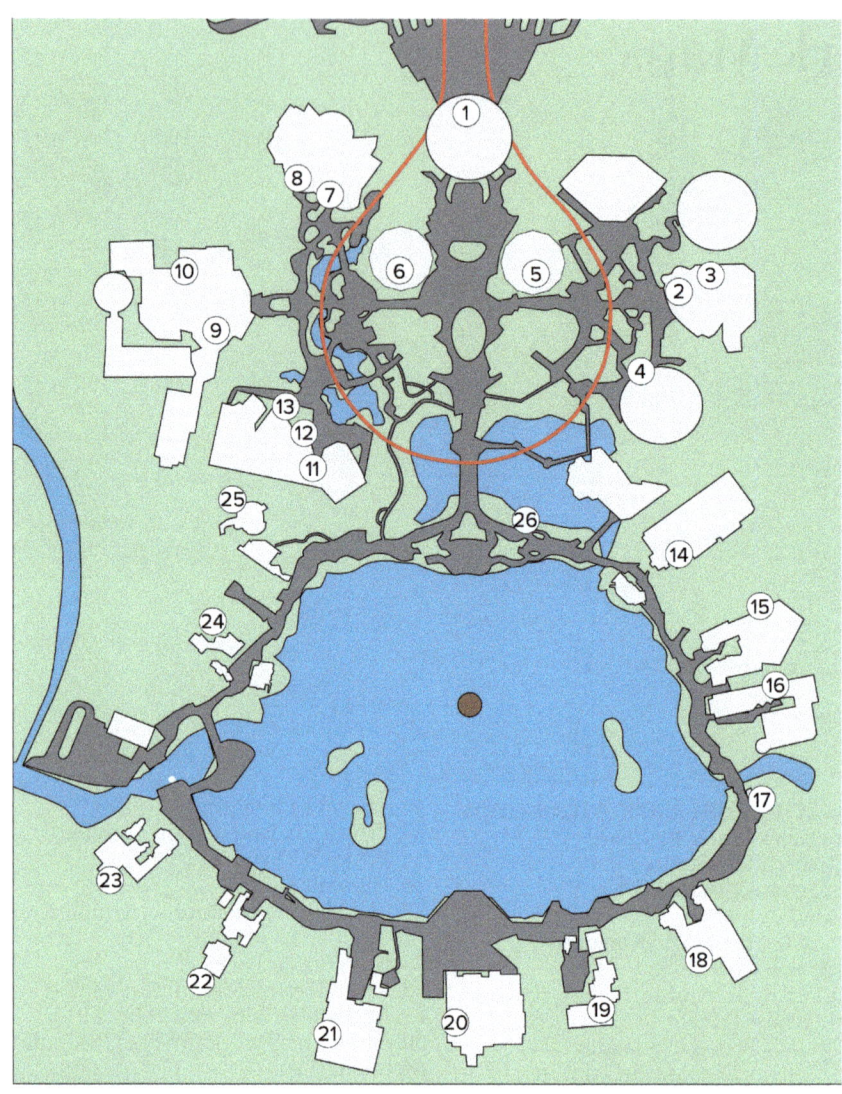

Epcot Attractions
1. Spaceship Earth (FP+)
2. Mission: SPACE (FP+)
3. Advanced Training Lab
4. Test Track (FP+)
5. Innoventions
6. Epcot Character Spot (FP+)
7. The Seas with Nemo and Friends (FP+)
8. Turtle Talk with Crush (FP+)
9. Soarin' Around the World (FP+)
10. Living with the Land (FP+)
11. Magic Eye Theater (FP+)
12. ImageWorks
13. Journey into Imagination with Figment (FP+)
14. Mexico – Grand Fiesta Tour starring the Three Caballeros
15. Norway – Frozen Ever After (FP+)
16. China – Reflections of China
17. Outpost
18. Germany
19. Italy
20. The American Adventure
21. Japan
22. Morocco
23. France – Impressions de France
24. United Kingdom
25. Canada – O' Canada
26. Character Meeting Location

Chapter Twenty-Nine | Park Maps

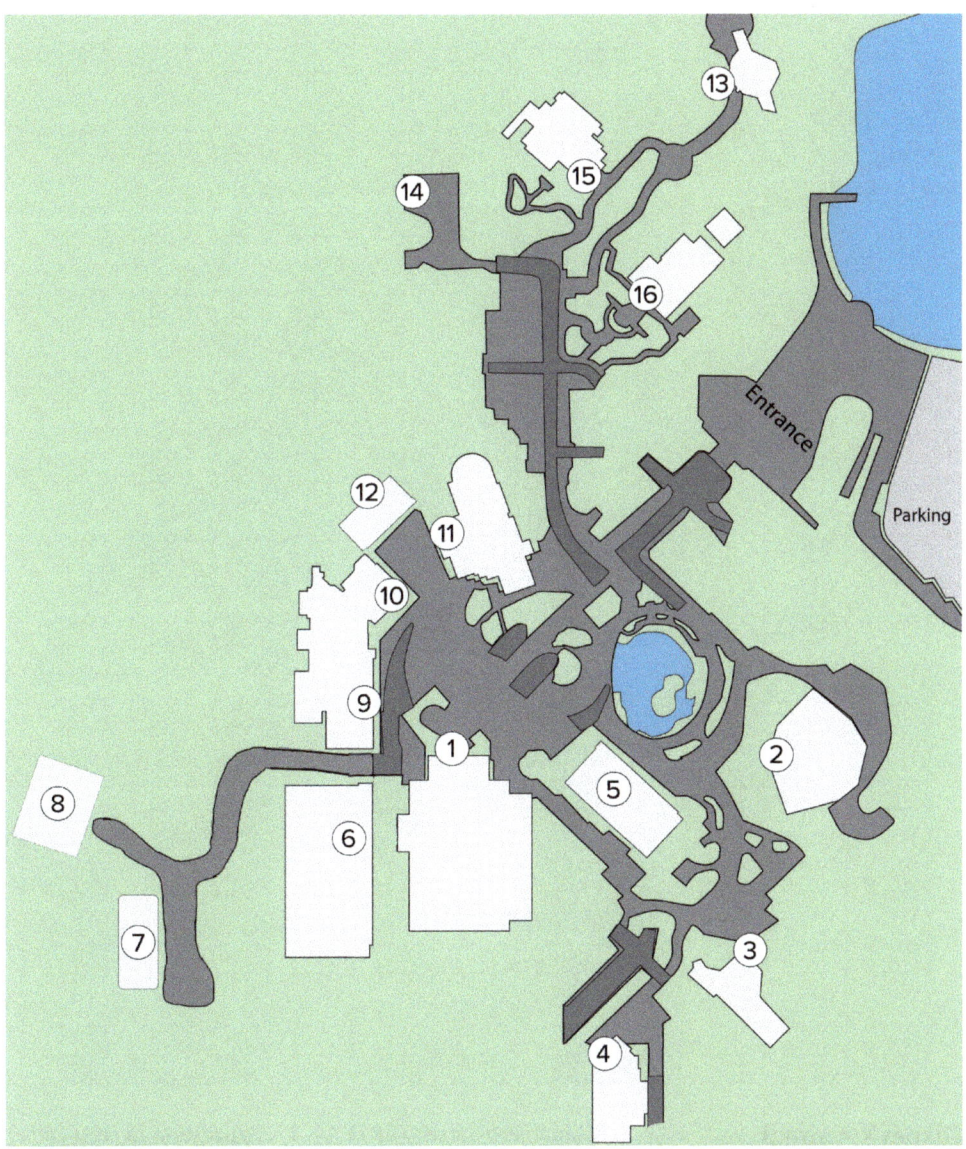

Disney's Hollywood Studios Attractions
1. Mickey & Minnie's Runaway Railway [Opens Fall 2019] (FP+)
2. Indiana Jones: Epic Stunt Spectacular (FP+)
3. Star Tours: The Adventures Continue (FP+)
4. MuppetVision 3D (FP+)
5. For the First Time in Forever: A Frozen Sing-Along Celebration (FP+)
6. Toy Story Midway Mania (FP+)
7. Alien Swirling Saucers (FP+)
8. Slinky Dog Dash
9. Walt Disney Presents (FP+)
10. Voyage of the Little Mermaid (FP+)
11. Disney Junior (FP+)
12. Star Wars: Launch Bay
13. Fantasmic (FP+)
14. Rock 'n' Roller Coaster: Starring Aerosmith (FP+)
15. The Twilight Zone: Tower of Terror (FP+)
16. Beauty and the Beast: Live on Stage (FP+)

The Independent Guide to Walt Disney World 2019 163

Chapter Twenty-Nine | Park Maps

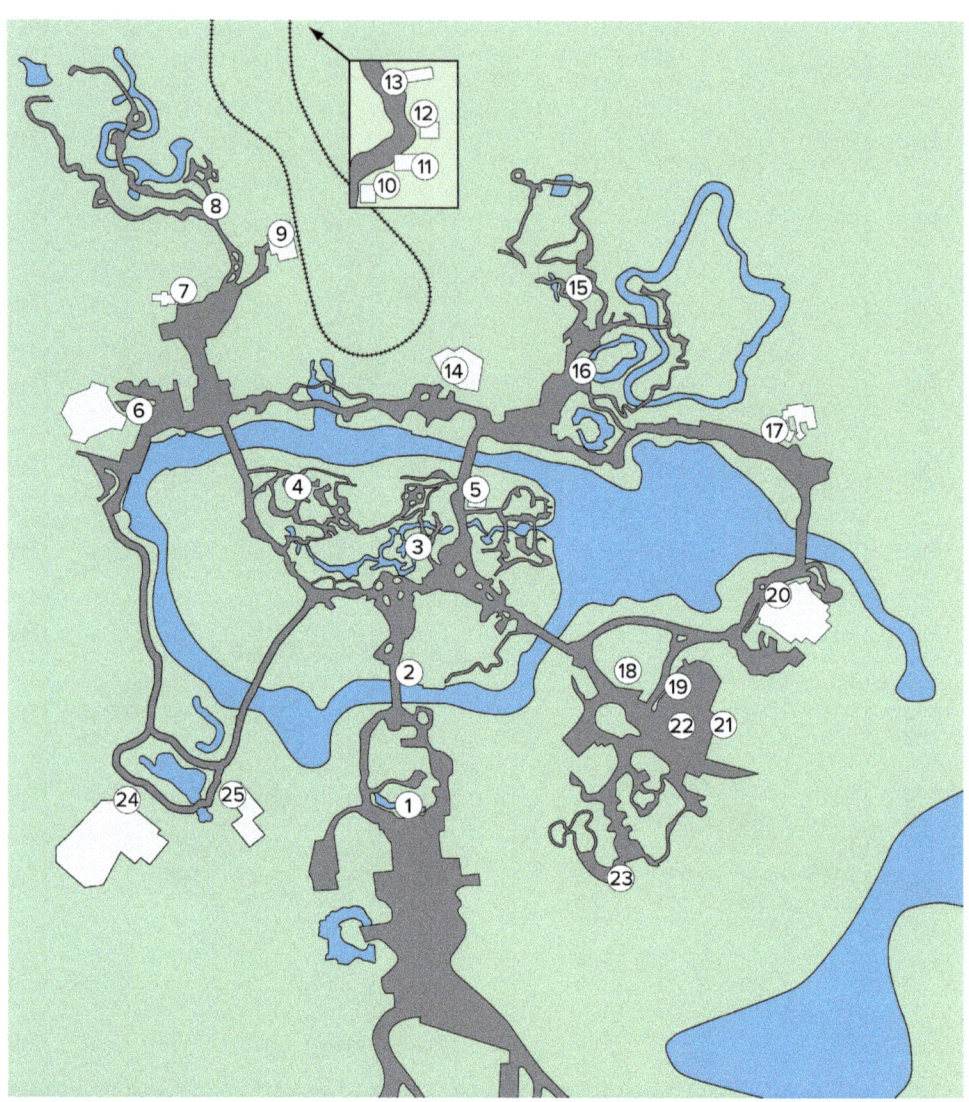

Disney's Animal Kingdom Park Attractions
1. The Oasis Exhibits
2. Wilderness Explorers
3. It's Tough to be a Bug! (FP+)
4. Discovery Island Trails
5. Adventurers Outpost (FP+)
6. Festival of the Lion King (FP+)
7. Kilimanjaro Safaris (FP+)
8. Gorilla Falls Exploration Trail
9 and 10. Wildlife Express Train
11. Habitat Habit!
12. Conservation Station
13. Affection Section
14. Up! A Great Bird Adventure (FP+)
15. Maharajah Jungle Trek
16. Kali River Rapids (FP+)
17. Expedition Everest (FP+)
18. The Boneyard
19. Fossil Fun Games
20. Finding Nemo: The Musical (FP+)
21. Primeval Whirl (FP+)
22. Triceratop Spin
23. DINOSAUR (FP+)
24. Avatar: Flight of Passage (FP+)
25. Na'vi River Journey (FP+)

Ingram Content Group UK Ltd.
Milton Keynes UK
UKHW022153170723
425309UK00010B/87